WESTERN CULTURE
TODAY AND TOMORROW

Joseph Cardinal Ratzinger

Western Culture
Today and Tomorrow

Addressing the Fundamental Issues

Translated by Michael J. Miller

Foreword by George Weigel

IGNATIUS PRESS   SAN FRANCISCO

Title of the Italian original:
Europa: I suoi fondamenti oggi e domani
© 2004 by Edizioni San Paolo, Cinisello Balsamo (Milan)
Second edition: 2005

English edition, titled *Europe Today and Tomorrow*
© 2007 by Libreria Editrice Vaticana
and Ignatius Press, San Francisco

Front cover photograph:
Sound and Light Show at Notre Dame de Paris
© by Pascal Deloche/Godong/Bridgeman Images

Cover design by John Herreid

Paperback edition printed in 2019 by Ignatius Press, San Francisco
Foreword © 2019 by Ignatius Press
Epilogue © 2019 by Libreria Editrice Vaticana
ISBN 978-1-62164-316-6 (PB)
ISBN 978-1-64229-087-5 (eBook)
Library of Congress Control Number 2019931439
Printed in the United States of America ∞

CONTENTS

FOREWORD

By George Weigel

Although historians of the future will likely remember his scholarly work for its important contributions to dogmatic theology and biblical commentary, Joseph Ratzinger was, for decades, an insightful, shrewd analyst of political modernity and its discontents. He had no particular interest in partisan politics. But good Augustinian that he was, this survivor of Nazi Germany understood that a state without justice is simply a band of robbers, as he put it to the Bundestag in 2012. Thus politics, for Ratzinger, was an exercise in moral reasoning. It was not just policy wonkery, and it was not just power games. And whenever it is reduced to mere technique, politics ends up producing the opposite of the justice and peace that are its purpose.

The essays collected in this slim but potent volume display Ratzinger's keen insight into the fundamental challenges confronting the late-twentieth- and early-twenty-first-century West. Those challenges, he insists, are fundamentally cultural in nature, before they are political or economic. Like his great partner, Pope Saint

John Paul II, Ratzinger knew that it takes a certain kind of people, living certain habits of mind and heart, to make democracy and free markets result in genuine human flourishing and social solidarity. Those habits—those virtues—are formed by a public moral culture; they are not products of the state or the market. And if the West finds itself steeped in political and economic discontent in the early twenty-first century, it had best look first to addressing its cultural malaise, if it is serious about fixing its politics and economics.

This is not, alas, a widespread conviction in twenty-first-century Europe, whose mandarins tend to think of public life in deeply secular and typically technocratic terms. Build the proper political and economic machinery, they imagine, and the machine will run by itself. Joseph Ratzinger knew that this notion was a snare and a delusion. And he knew that because he also knew that the civilizational project we call "the West" was, first and foremost, a cultural achievement with a history. And that history was forged by the interaction of Jerusalem, Athens, and Rome.

From Jerusalem—from biblical religion—what we know as "the West" learned that life is adventure, journey, pilgrimage. Mankind is going somewhere, and life is not repetitive, mindless cycles or one damn thing after another. The notion of history as pilgrimage was embodied in Israel's Exodus from Egypt; and that is why the Exodus is not only a determinative spiritual reality for Jews and Christians but *the* basic Western metaphor for both freedom and history.

From Athens—from classical philosophy—the West learned three things: there are truths inscribed into the world and into us; we can know those truths by reason; and, in knowing those truths, we come to know our obligations to ourselves and others. Classical philosophy also taught the West the crucial logical principle non-contradiction, which was essential in turning the basic proclamation of the Church—"Jesus is Lord"—into creed and doctrine. As Ratzinger once put it in a 1998 lecture to Asian theologians, it was providential that the first inculturation of the gospel took place where the principle of noncontradiction was secure. What would have happened if that first inculturation took place in a culture where it made perfect sense to say "Jesus is Lord" and "Jesus is not Lord" and mean both? The notion of truths embedded in the world and the principle of noncontradiction also explain why the West was the birthplace of modern science.

As for Rome, well, from the contentious history of the Roman Republic (and, indeed, from the better angels of imperial Rome), the West learned that the rule of law is morally and politically superior to the rule of brute force or coercion.

Jerusalem, Athens, and Rome, Ratzinger understood, were the three legs of the cultural stool on which what we call "the West" rests—and from that understanding, Ratzinger drew his analysis of the West's postmodern crisis. Nineteenth-century Western high culture kicked the Jerusalem leg out from under the stool, when its "atheist humanists" (as Henri de

Lubac dubbed them) declared the God of the Bible the enemy of human maturation and liberation. To many secularists, this detheologizing of culture seemed, not only obvious, but No Big Deal. Yet it turns out that, when you kick out the Jerusalem leg of the West's cultural support system, the Athenian leg gets wobbly. For absent the conviction that the God of the Bible imprinted something of his own "rationality" into a world created by the Logos (the Word or "reason" of God), reason begins to doubt its own ability to get at the truth of anything.

The first assaults on the capacity of reason to discern truth with certainty came from the likes of Immanuel Kant and David Hume; they now come from post-modernists who may concede "your truth" and "my truth" but nothing properly describable as *the* truth. And this, Ratzinger long taught, leads not just to intellectual muddle but to tyranny. For if there is only "your truth" and "my truth" and neither of us recognizes something called "*the* truth" that operates as a horizon of judgment, what happens when "your truth" and "my truth" collide? We have no way to adjudicate the argument. So you impose your power on me, or I impose my power on you.

And there we have what Ratzinger, in his memorable homily at the Mass for the Election of the Roman Pontiff in 2005, dubbed the "dictatorship of relativism"— the use of coercive state power to impose a relativistic moral order on all of society.

What would lead the West out of this slough of cultural despond?

Toward the end of this book, Ratzinger displays his skill at shedding light on public affairs through the prism of theology. After reiterating the importance to the West of the notion that God has imprinted something of the divine rationality on the world through the Logos, the Word of God, he reminds his Christian readers that God is not just Logos; God is also Love, and the divine love imprinted in the world calls us to solidarity, just as the divine reason calls us to truth. And that suggests a program for Christians seeking to renew a Western civilization in which aggressive secularism is leading to brittle cultural desiccation and the breakdown of social solidarity:

> We Christians must strive, together with all our fellow citizens, to give law and justice a moral foundation inspired by fundamental Christian ideas, however the [secular] individual may interpret their origins and harmonize them with his entire life.... [So] it is important for us to live out our own [Christian] heritage with vigor and purity, so that it might be made visible and effective, with all its intrinsic power of persuasion, to society as a whole.

The witness of Christian lives nobly lived is the beginning of reconversion (or, in many cases, conversion) of the West—and that return to the truths taught by the

God of the Bible is essential if the great Western civilizational project is not to crumble because of its current, postmodern incoherence. Joseph Ratzinger understood that danger long before many others. It would be well to attend to his prescription.

PREFACE

Europe is no less a current issue than it was when I published my first book on the subject (*Wendezeit für Europa?* 1991).[1] Over the course of the years, though, attention has been focused increasingly on the question of the general foundations of political action. Therefore the theme of Europe can be addressed now only within the context of the global challenges of our time. For my part, without seeking such occasions, I have been invited repeatedly during the past decade to give conferences on this subject. That is how the various chapters that together make up this little volume were produced.

Whereas the first essay attempts to clarify once again the question of what Europe is, what it can be, and what it ought to be, the other texts address the question of the criteria for correct political action against the background of the present European and global situation. Although it has not been possible in this anthology to avoid overlapping and repetition, I hope that a new

[1] *Wendezeit für Europa? Diagnosen und Prognosen zur Lage von Kirche und Welt* (Einsiedeln: Johannes Verlag, 1991); English trans.: *A Turning Point for Europe? The Church in the Modern World—Assessment and Forecast*, trans. Brian McNeil, C.R.V. (San Francisco: Ignatius Press, 1994).

collection of these individual statements will afford a better overview. On the other hand, I am fully aware of how inadequate the attempts presented in this volume are in dealing with the important questions of today that affect us all. Nevertheless, I hope that they can help to sharpen the vision of what is helpful and what is harmful.

JOSEPH RATZINGER
Rome, July 23, 2004
Feast of Saint Bridget of Sweden, Co-Patroness of Europe

PART ONE

WHAT IS EUROPE?

I

Europe:
Its Spiritual Foundations
Today and Tomorrow

Europe—what is it exactly? This question was asked
again and again, expressly, by Cardinal Józef Glemp in
one of the language circles of the Synod of Bishops on
Europe: Where does Europe begin, and where does
it end? Why, for example, does Siberia not belong to
Europe, even though it, too, is inhabited by Europeans, whose way of thinking and living is, furthermore,
quite European? And where do the frontiers of Europe
disappear to the south of the community of peoples
called Russia? And along what line of demarcation does
its boundary run in the Atlantic Ocean? Which islands
are *Europe*, and which ones are not, and why not? In

This text is essentially identical to a conference given in Berlin on Novem-
ber 28, 2000. For a conference that I gave at the invitation of the President
of the Senate of the Italian Republic, Marcello Pera, on May 13, 2004, I re-
worked the second part, taking into account some developments with regard to
the fundamental problems of the European Constitution.

those meetings it became perfectly clear that Europe is
a geographical concept only in a way that is entirely
secondary. Europe is not a continent that can be com-
prehended neatly in geographical terms; rather, it is a
cultural and historical concept.

1. The rise of Europe

This becomes quite clear if we try to go back to the
origins of Europe. Those who speak about the origin of
Europe usually cite Herodotus (ca. 484–425 B.C.), who
was no doubt the first to be acquainted with Europe as a
geographical concept; he defines it as follows: "For Asia,
with all the various tribes of barbarians that inhabit it, is
regarded by the Persians as their own; but Europe and
the Greek race they look on as distinct and separate."[1]
The boundaries of Europe itself are not specified, but it
is clear that lands which today are the nucleus of modern Europe lay entirely outside of the area considered
by the ancient historian. Indeed, with the establishment
of the Hellenistic states and the Roman Empire, a *continent* had been formed that became the basis for later
Europe, although it displayed entirely different boundaries: these were the lands surrounding the Mediterranean,
which by virtue of their cultural ties, by dint of trade and

[1] Herodotus, *History* I, 4, quoted from *The History of Herodotus*, trans. George
Rawlinson, Great Books Series, vol. 5 (Chicago: Encyclopaedia Britannica,
1990), 1–314, citation at page 2.

commerce, and by reason of their common political system formed all together a true and proper *continent*. Only the triumphant advance of Islam in the seventh and at the beginning of the eighth century drew a boundary across the Mediterranean and, so to speak, cut it in half, so that all that had been one continent until then was thenceforward subdivided into three continents: Asia, Africa, and Europe.

In the East the transformation of the world of antiquity took place more slowly than in the West: the Roman Empire with Constantinople as its center held out there—although under increasing pressure on its frontiers—until the fifteenth century.[2] Whereas around the year 700 the southern part of the Mediterranean fell completely outside of what had hitherto been a cultural continent, one notes at the same time an ever more vigorous extension toward the north. The *limes*, which until then had been a continental boundary line, disappears and opens up toward a new historical space that embraces Gaul, Germany, Britain as lands forming a true and proper nucleus, and it extends ever farther toward Scandinavia. In this process of displacing boundaries, the conceptual continuity with the preceding Mediterranean continent, although measured geographically in different terms, was assured by a theological interpretation

[2] An incisive and wide-ranging look at the formation of Europe, both in the geographic sense and as a system of values, is found in Peter Brown, *The Rise of Western Christendom: Triumph and Diversity*, A.D. *200–1000* (Oxford: Blackwell, 1995).

of history: in connection with the Book of Daniel, the Roman Empire—renewed and transformed by the Christian faith—was considered to be the final and permanent kingdom in the history of the world in general, and therefore the association of peoples and states that was taking shape was defined as the permanent *Sacrum Imperium Romanum* [Holy Roman Empire].

This process of a new historical and cultural definition was completed quite deliberately during the reign of Charlemagne, and here the ancient name of Europe emerged once again, in a significant variation: this term was now used precisely to designate the kingdom of Charlemagne, and it expressed simultaneously the awareness of the novelty and the continuity with which the new association of states presented itself as the political power in charge of the future. In charge of the future because it considered itself to be in continuity with the history of the world thus far and ultimately to be rooted in what lasts forever.[3]

Expressed in the self-understanding that was developing in this way was an awareness of being definitive and at the same time an awareness of having a mission.

It is true that the concept of Europe almost disappeared again after the end of the Carolingian rule and was preserved only in the language of the learned; it passed into the popular language only at the beginning of the

---

[3] Cf. H. Gollwitzer, "Europa, Abendland", in J. Ritter, ed., *Historisches Wörterbuch der Philosophie*, vol. 2 (Basel: Schwabe, 1971), 824–26; F. Prinz, *Von Konstantin zu Karl dem Grossen* (Düsseldorf: Artemis und Winkler, 2000).

modern era—no doubt in connection with the threat from the Turks, as a means of self-identification—and it became generally accepted in the eighteenth century. Independently of this history of the term "Europe", the establishment of the kingdom of the Franks, as the Roman Empire that had declined and was now reborn, signifies, indeed, a decisive step toward what we mean today when we speak of Europe.[4]

Of course we cannot deny that there is also a second root of Europe, of a non-Western Europe: as already noted, the Roman Empire in Byzantium had effectively resisted the storms of migrating peoples and of Islamic invasion. Byzantium always understood itself to be the true Rome; here, in fact, the empire had never declined, which was why it continued to assert a claim in its disputes with the other, western half of the empire. This eastern Roman Empire, too, extended farther to the north, until it reached the Slavic world, and it created its own Greco-Roman world, which differs from the Latin Europe of the West in its liturgy, its ecclesiastical constitution, its alphabet, and by its renunciation of Latin as the language of the learned.

To be sure, there were still sufficient unifying elements to make one continent out of these two worlds: in the first place, their common heritage of the Bible and of the early Church, which in both worlds, furthermore, referred beyond itself to a place of origin that now

---

[4] Cf. Gollwitzer, "Europa, Abendland", 826.

lay outside of Europe, namely, in Palestine; then the
same idea of empire, their common basic understanding of the Church, and hence also the common fund
of ideas concerning law and legal instruments; finally,
I should mention also monasticism, which among the
great movements of history had remained the essential
guarantor not only of cultural continuity, but above
all of fundamental religious and moral values, of man's
awareness of his ultimate destiny; and as a force prior
and superior to political authority, it became the source
of the rebirths that were necessary again and again.[5]

At the very heart of this common and essential eccle-
sial heritage, there was nevertheless a profound difference between the two Europes. Endre von Ivánka in
particular has underscored its importance: in Byzantium the empire and the Church appeared to be identified with each other; the emperor was the head of the
Church as well. He understood himself as the representative of Christ, and in connection with the figure of
Melchizedek, who was at the same time a king and a
priest (Gen 14:18), he bore the official title of "king and
priest" from the sixth century on.[6] Due to the fact that,
starting with Constantine, the emperor had departed

---

[5] From the wealth of literature on monasticism, I cite here only these: H.
Fischer, *Die Geburt der westlichen Zivilisation aus dem Geist des romanischen Mönch-
tums* (Munich: Kösel, 1969); F. Prinz, *Askese und Kultur: Vor- und frühbenedik-
tinisches Mönchtum an der Wiege Europas* (Munich: Beck, 1980).

[6] E. von Ivánka, *Rhomäerreich und Gottesvolk* (Freiburg and Munich: K.
Alber, 1968).

from Rome, it was possible in the old capital of the empire for the bishop of Rome to develop an autonomous position as the successor of Peter and supreme pastor of the Church. As early as the beginning of the Constantinian era, a duality of powers was taught there: in fact, the emperor and the pope had separate powers; neither one had complete authority. Pope Gelasius I (492–496) formulated the Western view in his famous letter to Emperor Anastasius and even more clearly in his fourth treatise, in which, contrary to the Byzantine typology of Melchizedek, he emphasized that the union of the powers was found exclusively in Christ: "He, indeed, because of human weakness (pride!), separated the two ministries for the following ages, so that no one might become proud" (chap. 11). For matters concerning eternal life the Christian emperors needed the priests (*pontifices*), and the latter, in turn, abided by the imperial ordinances in the course of temporal affairs. In worldly matters, the priests had to follow the laws of the emperor who had been placed in office by a divine decree, whereas he had to submit to the priest in sacred matters.[7] Thereby a separation and distinction

---

[7] Primary sources and secondary literature can be found in U. Duchrow, *Christenheit und Weltverantwortung* (Stuttgart: Klett, 1970), 328ff. There is a wealth of material on this subject in Hugo Rahner, *Church and State in Early Christianity*, trans. Leo Donald David (San Francisco: Ignatius Press, 1992). Stephan Horn brought to my attention an important passage by Leo the Great contained in a letter dated May 22, 452, from the Pope to the Emperor, in which he refutes the famous canon 28 of Chalcedon (concerning the primatial position of Constantinople vis-à-vis Rome, based on the presence of the seat

of powers was introduced, which became extremely important in the subsequent development of Europe and which laid the foundations, so to speak, for what is distinctively typical of the West.

Since the totalitarian impulse always remained alive in both parties, despite this distinction, along with the desire to place one's own power above the other, this principle of separation also became the source of infinite sufferings. The correct way of seeing and applying it, politically and from a religious perspective, still remains a fundamental problem for the Europe of today and tomorrow.

2. At the turn of the modern era

If on the basis of what has been said here we can consider the rise of the Carolingian Empire, on the one hand, and the continuation of the Roman Empire in

---

of the empire in the former city): "Habeat sicut optamus Constantinopolitana civitas gloriam suam, et protegente Dei dextera diuturno clementiae vestrae fruatur imperio, alia tamen ratio est rerum saecularium alia divinarum, nec praeter illam petram quam Dominus in fundamento posuit stabilis erit ulla constructio" (LME II [37] 55, 52–56; cf. ACO II/IV, p. 56) [We wish that the city of Constantinople may have its proper glory and, under the protection of God's right hand, might enjoy the perpetual rule of your clemency; nevertheless, the scheme of worldly things is different from that of things divine, nor will there be any lasting building apart from that rock which the Lord placed as the foundation]. On this problem, see also A. Michel, "Der Kampf um das politische oder petrinische Prinzip der Kirchenführung", in A. Grillmeier and H. Bacht, *Das Konzil von Chalkedon*, vol. 2, *Entscheidung um Chalkedon* (Würzburg: Echter, 1953), 491–562; and the essay by Thomas O. Martin on canon 28 of Chalcedon in the same volume (433–58).

Byzantium and its mission to the Slavic people, on the other, as the true and proper birth of the *continent* of Europe, the beginning of the modern era meant a turning point for both Europes, a radical change that concerns both the nature of this continent and its geographic contours. In 1453 Constantinople was conquered by the Turks. O. Hiltbrunner comments laconically on this event: "The last ... scholars emigrated ... to Italy and transmitted to the humanists of the Renaissance their knowledge of the original Greek texts; but the East sank into an absence of culture."[8] This statement is formulated in a way that is a bit too harsh, for in fact even the reign of the Ottoman dynasty had its culture; but it is true that the Greco-Christian, *European* culture of Byzantium came to an end. Thus one of the two wings of Europe was in danger of disappearing as a result, but the Byzantine heritage was not dead. Moscow declared itself to be the Third Rome and now founded its own patriarchate based on the notion of a second *translatio imperii* [transfer of the seat of the empire] thus presenting itself as a new metamorphosis of the *Sacrum Imperium* [Holy Empire], as a distinct form of Europe, which nonetheless remained united with the West and was increasingly oriented to it, until Peter the Great attempted to turn it into a Western country. This displacement of

[8] O. Hiltbrunner, *Kleines Lexikon der Antike* (Bern and Munich: Francke, 1950), 102.

Byzantine Europe toward the north brought with it the development that now the boundaries of the continent, too, began to move extensively toward the east. Determining the Ural Mountains as the boundary is completely arbitrary; in any case the region to the east of them became more and more a sort of substructure of Europe, being neither Asia nor Europe, substantially shaped by the acting subject Europe, without participating itself, however, in its subject character; instead it was an object and not responsible for its own history. Perhaps that describes, in summary form, the nature of a colonial state.

With regard to Byzantine (not Western) Europe at the beginning of the modern era, therefore, we can speak of a twofold development: on the one hand, there was the dissolution of ancient Byzantium in its historical continuity with the Roman Empire; on the other hand, this second Europe obtained in Moscow a new center and expanded its borders to the east, so as to set up finally in Siberia a sort of preliminary colonial structure.

During that same period we can note in the West also a twofold process with a remarkable historic significance. A large part of the Germanic world separated itself from Rome; a new, *enlightened* form of Christianity arose, so that henceforth a line of demarcation ran through the *West*, which clearly formed another cultural *limes*, a *boundary* between two different ways of thinking and interrelating. Of course, within the Protestant world there was a break, in the first place between Lutherans

and the Reformed churches (which includes Method-
ists and Presbyterians), while the Church of England
attempted to devise a middle way between Catholics
and Evangelicals; to this was added later the difference
between Christianity in the form of a State church,
which became typical of Europe, and the free churches
that found refuge in North America—a subject to which
we will have to return in our discussion.

For now, let us examine the second event, which is
essential to the character of the modern era, as opposed
to the situation in what at one time was Latin [that is,
Western] Europe: the discovery of America. To the
expansion of Europe toward the east, thanks to the progressive extension of Russia toward Asia, corresponds
the transplanting of Europe outside of its geographical
boundaries in the world beyond the Atlantic Ocean,
which is now called America. The subdivision of Europe
into a Latin-Catholic half and a Germanic-Protestant
half was transferred to this part of the earth occupied
by Europe and had its repercussions there. America,
too, became at first an extension of Europe, a *colony*,
but it established its own character as an acting subject
at the time of the uprising in Europe that resulted from
the French Revolution. From the nineteenth century
on, America, although profoundly shaped by its European origins, nevertheless has stood opposite Europe as
a distinct subject.

In our attempt to discover the deeper, more interior
identity of Europe through this historical survey, we

have looked now at two fundamental turning points
in history: first, the disintegration of the old Mediterranean continent under the influence of the continent
of the *Sacrum Imperium*, located farther to the north, in
which *Europe* took shape beginning with the Carolingian period as a Latin and Western world; alongside
this was the continuation of the old Rome in Byzantium, with its extension toward the Slavic world. The
second transition that we have observed was the fall
of Byzantium and, on the one hand, the subsequent
movement of the Christian idea of empire toward the
north and the east and, on the other hand, the internal division of Europe into two worlds, one Germanic
and Protestant and the other Latin and Catholic, and
furthermore the emigration to America, to which this
division was transferred and which ultimately established itself as an independent historical subject that
stood opposite Europe. Now we must take into consideration a third turning point, for which the French
Revolution was the signal light seen around the world.
It is true that the Holy Roman Empire, as a political
reality, was already thought to be falling apart from the
late medieval period on and had become increasingly
fragile, even as a valid and unquestionable interpretation of history, but only now [in the late eighteenth
century] did this spiritual framework go to pieces for-
mally as well—that spiritual framework without which
Europe could not have been formed. This was a process of considerable importance, both from the political

and from the conceptual point of view. In the realm of ideas, this meant that the sacred foundation for history and for the existence of the State was rejected; history was no longer gauged on the basis of an idea of a pre-existent God who shaped it; the State was henceforth considered in purely secular terms, founded on reason and on the will of the citizens.

For the very first time in history, a purely secular State arose, which abandoned and set aside the divine guarantee and the divine ordering of the political sector, considering them a mythological world view, and it declared God himself to be a private affair, that did not play a role in public life or the formation of the popular will. The latter was seen now solely as a matter of reason, by which God did not appear to be clearly knowable; religion and faith in God belonged to the realm of feelings and not to that of reason. God and his will ceased to be relevant in public life.

In this way a new type of schism arose at the end of the eighteenth and the beginning of the nineteenth century, the seriousness of which we now perceive more and more clearly. There is no German word for it, because in that part of Europe it spread more slowly. In the Romance languages it is described as a division between *Christians* and *secular persons* [Italian, *laici*, French, *laïcs*: "laymen"]. This rift ran through the Latin nations during the last two centuries as a deep breach, whereas Protestant Christianity at first had no trouble allowing room within itself for liberal and

Enlightenment ideas, without that necessarily destroying the framework of a broad, basic Christian consensus.
The former idea of power disappeared, yielding to a
political realism consisting of a recognition of the fact
that now nations and states had become identifiable as
such through the formation of uniform linguistic regions
and that these appeared as the unique and true subjects
of history and therefore attained a status higher than they
had had previously. The subject of history was now plural, and the explosive and dramatic consequences of this
are evident in the fact that the great European nations
considered themselves entrusted with a universal mission, which necessarily led to conflicts among them, the
deadly impact of which we have painfully experienced
in the century that just ended.

3. The universalization of European culture and its crises

Finally we must also consider here a later process by
which the history of the last several centuries clearly
crossed over into a new world. Whereas the two halves
of the old Europe, before the modern era, had known
essentially only one opponent that it had to confront in
a life-or-death battle, namely, the Islamic world, and
whereas the advent of the modern era had brought the
expansion toward America and toward parts of Asia that
did not have their own large autonomous cultural units,

now emigration began toward the two continents that until then had been only marginally affected: Africa and Asia, and now there was likewise an attempt to turn them into annexes of Europe, into *colonies*. To a certain extent this, too, was successful, inasmuch as Asia and Africa today follow the ideal of a world shaped by technology and material comforts, so that there, too, the ancient religious traditions are facing a crisis, and strains of purely secular thought are dominating public life more and more.

But there is also a contrary effect: the rebirth of Islam is not only connected with the new material wealth of Islamic countries; it is also nourished by the awareness that Islam is capable of offering a valid spiritual basis for the life of the peoples, a basis that seems to have slipped out of the hands of old Europe, which thus, notwithstanding its continued political and economic power, is increasingly viewed as a declining culture condemned to fade away.

The great religious traditions of Asia, too, especially its mystical element, which finds expression in Buddhism, are rising as spiritual powers in contrast to a Europe that is denying its religious and moral foundations. The optimism concerning the triumph of the European way that Arnold Toynbee was still able to maintain at the beginning of the 1960s today seems strangely outdated: "Of the twenty-eight cultures that we have identified ... eighteen are dead and nine of the ten left—i.e., all except our own—appear to be mortally wounded."[9] Who would repeat those same words today? And what, in the first place, *is* this culture of ours that has remained? Is European culture perhaps the civilization of technology and commerce that has spread victoriously through the entire world? Or maybe that was born, instead, from the end of that ancient European culture as a post-European phenomenon. I see here a paradoxical coincidence: with the triumph of the post-European technological-secular world, with the globalization of its way of life and its manner of thinking, one gets the impression everywhere in the world, but especially in the strictly non-European worlds of Asia and Africa, that the very world of European values—the things upon which Europe bases its identity, its culture and its faith—has arrived at its end and has actually already left the scene; that now the hour has come for the value systems of other worlds, of pre-Columbian America, of Islam, of Asian mysticism.

Europe, precisely in this hour of its greatest success, seems to have become hollowed out, paralyzed in a certain sense by a crisis of its circulatory system, a crisis that endangers its life, which depends, so to speak, on

[9] Arnold Joseph Toynbee, *A Study of History*, vol. 2, *Geneses of Civilizations* (London: Oxford Univ. Press, H. Milford, 1934); quoted from the German edition, *Der Gang der Weltgeschichte II: Kulturen im Übergang* (Zürick, Stuttgart, and Vienna: Europa-Verlag, 1958), p. 370, as cited in J. Holdt, *Hugo Rahner: Sein geschichtstheologisches Denken* (Paderborn: Schöningh, 1997), 53. In particular, Holdt's section entitled "Philosophische Besinnung auf das Abendland" [Philosophical Meditation on the West] (52–61) furnishes important materials for the question concerning Europe.

transplants, which then, however, cannot help undermining its identity. This interior dwindling of the spiritual strength that once supported it is accompanied by the fact that Europe appears to be on the way out ethnically as well. There is a strange lack of will for the future. Children, who are the future, are seen as a threat to the present; it is thought that they take away something of our life. They are perceived, not as a hope, but rather as a limitation on the present. This invites a comparison with the decline of the Roman Empire: it was still functioning as a great historical context, but in practice it was already living off of those who would eventually break it up, because it no longer had any vital energy of its own.

With that we have arrived at the problems of the present day. Concerning the possible future of Europe there are two contrasting diagnoses. On the one hand, there is the thesis of Oswald Spengler, who thought that he could ascertain among the great civilizations a sort of natural law: there is the moment of birth, the gradual growth, then the flowering of a culture, its slow decline, aging and death. Spengler illustrates his thesis in an impressive manner, with documentation taken from the history of various cultures, in which one can glimpse this law of natural development. His thesis was that the West has arrived at its final epoch, which runs inexorably toward the death of this cultural continent, despite all efforts to avert it. Naturally Europe can hand on its gifts to a new, emerging culture, as has already happened in preceding instances of the decline of a culture; but as a subject with its own identity, its heyday is already past.

This thesis, which was labeled "biologistic", met with impassioned opposition in the period between the two world wars, especially in Catholic circles; it was impressively countered by Arnold Toynbee, who relied, however, on presuppositions that do not find much of a hearing today.[10] Toynbee highlights the difference between material and technological progress, on the one hand, and real progress, on the other, which he defines as spiritualization. He admits that the West—the *Western world*—is in the midst of a crisis, the cause of which he sees in the fact that it has fallen from religion to the worship of technology, of the nation, of militarism. Ultimately the crisis for him is one of secularism.

If we know the cause of the crisis, it is possible also to show the way to a cure: we have to reintroduce the religious factor, which comprises, in his opinion, the religious heritage of all cultures, but especially "what has remained of Western Christianity".[11] In contrast to the biologistic view, he proposes a voluntaristic view that

---

[10] O. Spengler, *The Decline of the West*, authorized translation with notes by Charles Francis Atkinson (New York: Knopf, 1939). On the debate surrounding his thesis, see the chapter "Die abendländische Bewegung zwischen den Weltkriegen" [The Western movement between the World Wars], in Holdt, *Hugo Rahner*, 13–17. Confronting Spengler's thought was also a recurring theme in the work of fundamental moral philosophy written during the period between the two wars by T. Steinbüchel, *Die philosophische Grundlegung der katholischen Sittenlehre* (Düsseldorf: Schwamm, 1938; 3rd ed., 1947).

[11] Cf. Holdt, *Hugo Rahner*, 54.

places its bets on the powers of creative minorities and on exceptional individuals. The question that arises is: Is this diagnosis correct? And if so, is it within our power to reintroduce the religious element, in a synthesis of residual Christianity and the religious heritage of mankind? Ultimately the question of who was right—Spengler or Toynbee—remains open, because we cannot see into the future. But independently of that debate, we are obliged to ask ourselves what can guarantee the future and what is capable of keeping alive the intrinsic identity of Europe through all the historical metamorphoses. Or to put it even more simply: What is there, today and tomorrow, that promises human dignity and a life in conformity with it?

To find an answer, we must turn our attention once again to the present day and at the same time keep in mind its historical roots. In the preceding discussion we stopped at the French Revolution and the nineteenth century. At that time two new *European* models in particular had developed. In the Latin nations [that is, where the Romance languages were spoken] there was the laicist model: the State was quite distinct from the religious organizations, which were relegated to the private sphere. The State itself renounced any religious basis and claimed to be founded solely on reason and on its own intuitions. When confronted with the frailty of reason, these systems have proved to be fragile and have easily fallen victim to dictatorships; they survive, actually, only because parts of the old moral consciousness continue to exist, even without the previous social foundations, making possible a basic moral consensus. On the other hand, in the Germanic [and Anglo-Saxon] world, there were different models of Church and State, derived from liberal Protestantism; in them an enlightened Christian religion, essentially understood as morality—together with forms of worship guaranteed by the State—assured a moral consensus and a broad religious foundation, to which the faiths other than the State religion had to conform. This model in Great Britain, in the Scandinavian states, and at first even in Germany ruled by the Prussians, for a long time assured national and social cohesiveness. In Germany, however, the collapse of the Christianity of the Prussian State created a void, which then also left room for a dictatorship. Today State churches everywhere have suffered from attrition: religious bodies derived from the State no longer provide any moral force, whereas the State itself cannot create moral force but rather must presuppose it and build upon it.

Somewhere between these two models we find the United States of America, which, on the one hand—formed on the basis of free churches—started out from a rigid dogma of [Church-State] separation. On the other hand, beyond the particular denominations, the nation was shaped nonetheless by a basic Protestant Christian consensus that was not hammered out in doctrinal-confessional terms but was associated with a special awareness of its mission, in its dealings with the rest of the world, as a religious example and thus gave significant public weight to the religious factor, which as a prepolitical and suprapolitical force managed to have influence on political life. Of course we cannot overlook here the fact that in the United States, too, the disintegration of the Christian heritage advances unceasingly, while at the same time the rapid increase of the Hispanic population and the presence of traditional religions from all parts of the world complete the picture. Perhaps we should observe here, too, that certain circles in the United States are giving plenty of support to the Protestantization of Latin America and thus promoting the break-up of the Catholic Church by means of free church structures; they are convinced that the Catholic Church is not in a position to guarantee a stable political and economic system and hence is incapable of functioning as a teacher of nations, whereas it is expected that the model of the free churches will make possible a moral consensus and a democratic formation of the public will, similar to those found in the United States. To complicate the picture further, it must be admitted that today the Catholic Church constitutes the largest religious community in the United States and that in her life of faith she stands up resolutely for her Catholic identity; yet with regard to the relationship between Church and politics, American Catholics have accepted the traditions of the free churches, in the sense that it is precisely a Church unaffiliated with the State that best guarantees the moral foundations of the whole society, so that promoting the democratic ideal appears to be a moral duty that is profoundly in keeping with the faith. In such a position we have good reason to see a continuation, adapted to the times, of the model of Pope Gelasius, of whom I spoke earlier.

Let us turn to Europe. To the two models about which I spoke before, a third was added in the nineteenth century, namely, socialism, which soon subdivided into two different paths, the totalitarian and the democratic. Starting from its initial premise, democratic socialism was able to become part of the two existing models, as a salutary counterbalance to the radical liberal positions, enriching and correcting them. It proved, furthermore, to be something that transcended denominational affiliations: in England it was the party of the Catholics, who could not feel at home either in the Protestant-conservative camp or among the liberals. In Germany under Kaiser Wilhelm, too, many Catholic centrists felt closer to democratic socialism than to the rigidly Prussian and Protestant conservative forces. In many respects democratic socialism was and is close to Catholic social doctrine; in any case, it contributed considerably toward the formation of a social consciousness.

The totalitarian model, in contrast, was associated with a rigidly materialistic and atheistic philosophy of history: history was understood deterministically as a process of advancement that passed through a religious and then a liberal phase so as to arrive at the absolute and definitive society, in which religion becomes a superfluous relic from the past and the business of material production and trade is able to guarantee happiness for all. The scientific appearance of this theory conceals an intolerant dogmatism: spirit is the product of matter; morals are the product of circumstances and must be defined and practiced according to the goals of society: everything that fosters the coming of that final state of happiness and morality. Here the values that had built Europe are completely overturned. Even worse, there is a rupture here with the complex moral tradition of mankind: there are no longer any values apart from the goals of progress; at a given moment everything can be permitted and even necessary, can be "moral" in a new sense of the word. Even man can become an instrument; the individual does not matter. The future alone becomes the terrible deity that rules over everyone and everything.

Meanwhile the Communist systems have foundered, above all because of their false economic dogmatism. But too often people ignore the fact that the more fundamental reason for their shipwreck was their contempt for human rights, their subjection of morality to the demands of the system and to their promises for the future. The real catastrophe they left behind is not of an economic sort; it consists, rather, in the drying up of souls, in the destruction of moral conscience. I see as an essential problem in our day, for Europe and for the world, the fact that the economic failure is never disputed, and therefore the former Communists have become economic liberals almost without hesitation, whereas the moral and religious problem, which was really at stake, is almost completely dismissed. Nevertheless, the complex problems left behind by Marxism continue to exist today. The loss of man's primordial certainties about God, about himself, and about the universe—the loss of an awareness of intangible moral values—is still our problem, especially today, and it can lead to the self-destruction of the European consciousness, which we must begin to consider—independently of Spengler's vision of decline—as a real danger.[12]

4. What point have we reached today?

Thus we find ourselves facing the question: Where do we go from here? In the violent upheavals of our time, is there a European identity that has a future and to which we can commit ourselves with all our might? I am not prepared to enter into a detailed discussion of the future European Constitution. I would just like to note briefly the foundational moral elements that in my opinion should not be missing from it.

The first element is the "unconditional character" of human dignity and human rights, which must be

---

[12] In this regard we must cite the following words by E. Chargaff: "Where everyone is free to take the lion's share, for example in the free market, the result is the society of Marsia, a society of bloody corpses" (E. Chargaff, *Ein zweites Leben: Autobiographische und andere Texte* [Stuttgart: Klett-Cotta, 1955], 168).

presented as values that are prior to any governmental jurisdiction. These fundamental rights are not created by the legislator or conferred upon the citizens, "but rather they exist in their own right; they must always be respected by the legislator and are given to him previously as values of a higher order."[13] This validity of human dignity, prior to any political action or decision, is ultimately derived from the Creator: only God can establish values that are based on the nature of man and are inviolable. The fact that there are values that cannot be manipulated by anyone is the real guarantee of our liberty and of human greatness: Christian faith sees in this the mystery of the Creator and of the status that he has conferred upon man as the image of God.

Now today almost nobody will deny outright the precedence of human dignity and fundamental human rights over any political decision; the horrors of Nazism and of its racist theory are still too recent. But within the pragmatic sphere of so-called progress in medicine there are very real threats to these values: whether we think of cloning or of the preservation of human fetuses for the purpose of research and organ donation or of the whole field of genetic manipulation—no one can mistake the gradual atrophy of respect for human dignity that threatens us here. Added to this is a burgeoning traffic in human persons, new forms

[13] G. Hirsch, "Ein Bekenntnis zu den Grundwerten" [An affirmation of fundamental values], in *Frankfurter Allgemeine Zeitung*, October 12, 2000.

of slavery, and trafficking in human organs for transplantation. *Good ends* are always adduced to justify the unjustifiable.

In summary: to establish in writing the value and dignity of man, of liberty, equality, and solidarity, along with the fundamental declarations of democracy and of a state governed by law, implies an image of man, a moral option, and a concept of law that are by no means obvious but that are actually fundamental factors in the identity of Europe. These constitutive elements, along with their concrete consequences, ought to be guaranteed in the future European Constitution; certainly they can be defended only if a corresponding moral consciousness is continually formed anew.

A second area in which the European identity appears is marriage and the family. Monogamous marriage, as a fundamental structure of the relation between man and woman and at the same time as the basic cell in the formation of the larger community, was modeled on the basis of biblical faith. This gave Europe, both in the West and in the East, its particular face and its particular humanity, also and especially because the pattern of fidelity and self-denial depicted there had to be won again and again, by many toils and sufferings. Europe would no longer be Europe if this fundamental cell of its social edifice were to disappear or if its nature were to be changed. We all know how marriage and the family are threatened—on the one hand, by the voiding of its indissolubility as a result of increasingly easy

forms of divorce and, on the other hand, through a new
kind of behavior that is becoming ever more widespread: the cohabitation of a man and a woman without
the legal form of marriage. In tawdry contrast with all
that is the demand for domestic partnerships between
homosexuals, who now paradoxically are demanding a
legal form that would have to be equated more or less
with marriage. This trend departs completely from the
moral history of mankind, which, despite all the diversity in the legal form of marriage, nevertheless always
recognized that said marriage, by its very nature, is the
exclusive association of a man and a woman that is
open to children and thus to the family. Here we are
dealing, not with discrimination, but with the question
of what the human person is, as man or as woman,
and of how the common life of man and woman can
acquire a legal form. If, on the one hand, their living
together becomes increasingly detached from juridical forms and, on the other hand, homosexual unions
are seen more and more as having the same status as
marriage, then we are confronted with a disintegration
of the image of man, which can only have extremely
serious consequences.

My final point is the religious question. I do not wish
to enter here into the complex discussions of the last few
years. I would like instead to highlight just one aspect
that is fundamental to all cultures: respect for what is
sacred to someone else and, in particular, respect for
the sacred in the more exalted sense, for God, something

we are allowed to expect even in a person who is not disposed to believe in God. Where this respect is violated, something essential in a society is lost. In our society today, thank God, anyone who dishonors the faith of Israel, its image of God, or its great personages is censured. Anyone who insults the Qur'an and the fundamental beliefs of Islam is censured, too. On the other hand, where Christ and what is sacred to Christians are concerned, suddenly freedom of opinion appears to be the highest good, and to limit it would be to endanger tolerance and freedom in general or to destroy them outright. Freedom of opinion, however, discovers its limit in the fact that it cannot destroy the honor and the dignity of someone else; denying or destroying human rights is not freedom.

Here we notice a self-hatred in the Western world that is strange and that can be considered pathological; yes, the West is making a praiseworthy attempt to be completely open to understanding foreign values, but it no longer loves itself; from now on it sees in its own history only what is blameworthy and destructive, whereas it is no longer capable of perceiving what is great and pure. In order to survive, Europe needs a new—and certainly a critical and humble—acceptance of itself, that is, if it *wants* to survive. Multiculturalism, which is continually and passionately encouraged and promoted, is sometimes little more than the abandonment and denial of what is one's own, flight from one's own heritage. But multiculturalism cannot exist without shared constants, without points of reference based on one's own values. It surely cannot exist without respect for what is sacred. Part of it is approaching with respect the things that are sacred to others, but we can do this only if what is sacred, God himself, is not foreign to us. Of course, we can and must learn from what is sacred to others, but given this encounter with others and precisely for those others it is our duty to nourish within ourselves a respect in the presence of what is sacred and to manifest the face of God who has appeared to us: the God who has compassion on the poor and the weak, on widows and orphans, on the stranger; the God who is so humane that he himself became man, a suffering man, who by suffering together with us gives dignity and hope to pain.

If we do not do this, we not only deny the identity of Europe, but we also deprive others of a service to which they have a right. For the cultures of the world, the absolute secularity that has been taking shape in the West is something profoundly foreign. They are convinced that a world without God has no future. And so multiculturalism itself calls us to come to our senses and to look deep within ourselves again.

We do not know how things will go in Europe in the future. The Charter of Fundamental Rights [of the European Union] may be a first step, a sign that Europe is consciously looking again for its soul. In this regard we must say that Toynbee was correct, that the destiny of a society always depends on creative minorities.

Believing Christians should think of themselves as one such creative minority and contribute to Europe's recovery of the best of its heritage and thus to the service of all mankind.

2

Reflections on Europe

What is Europe? What can and should it be in the overall framework of the historical situation in which we
find ourselves at the beginning of the third Christian
millennium? After the Second World War, the search
for a common identity and a common goal for Europe
entered into a new phase. After two suicidal wars, which
during the first half of the twentieth century had devastated Europe and involved the entire world, it had
become clear that all European states were losers in that
terrible drama and that something had to be done to
avoid any further repetition of it. In the past, Europe
had always been a continent of contrasts, agitated by
multiple conflicts. The nineteenth century had then
brought the formation of nation-states, whose clashing
interests had given a new dimension to the destructive

Conference given on September 8, 2001, in Cernobbio (Como). In the
presence of important representatives of the economic and political world, I
wanted, without offering ready-made solutions, to highlight the aspects that
cannot be reduced to economic questions as a challenge for contemporary
politics.

opposition. The work of European unification was defined essentially by two motives. As opposed to the divisive nationalistic movements and hegemonic ideologies that had radicalized the conflict in World War II, the common cultural, moral, and religious heritage of Europe was supposed to shape the conscience of its nations, thus revealing the way of peace as the common identity of all its peoples and a common path toward the future. They were seeking a European identity that would not dissolve or deny the national identities, but rather unite them at a higher level of unity into one community of peoples. Their common history would have to be employed to advantage as a peacemaking force. There is no doubt that among the founding fathers of European unification the Christian heritage was considered the nucleus of this historical identity—of course, not in its denominational forms; what is common to all Christians, however, seemed to be discernible beyond the denominational boundaries as a unifying force for action in the secular world. It did not even appear to be incompatible with the great moral ideals of the Enlightenment, which had given prominence, so to speak, to the rational dimension of the Christian reality and, transcending all the historical oppositions, certainly seemed to be compatible with the fundamental ideals of the Christian history of Europe. This general intuition has never been made quite clear in all its particular details with supporting evidence; in that sense there are still some problems here that require deeper study. At the time when the movement first began, nevertheless, the conviction that the major components of the European heritage were compatible was stronger than the problems that existed in that regard.

Besides this historical and moral dimension at the beginning of European unification, there was also a second motive. European dominion over the world, which had been expressed above all in the colonial system and in the resulting economic and political ties, was finished forever with the conclusion of the Second World War. In this sense Europe as a whole had lost the war. The United States of America set up camp now on the stage of world history as the ruling power, but even defeated Japan became an economic power, and finally the Soviet Union, together with its satellites, constituted an empire on which the third-world nations in particular sought to rely, as opposed to America and Western Europe. In this new situation the individual European states could no longer present themselves as dialogue partners of equal status. The unification of their interests in a common European structure became necessary if Europe were to continue to have any weight in world politics. The national interests had to join together in a common European interest. Along with the search for a common identity derived from their history that would foster peace came an affirmation of common interests; then there was the will to become an economic power, which is of course the prerequisite for political power. Over the course of the developments in the last fifty years, this second aspect of European unification has become ever more dominant, indeed, almost exclusively influential. The common European currency is the clearest expression of this orientation in the work of European unification: Europe appears as an economic and monetary union, which as such participates in the formation of history and lays claim to a space of its own.

Karl Marx proposed the thesis that religions and philosophies are merely ideological superstructures for economic relationships. This does not entirely correspond to the truth; one would have to speak instead about a reciprocal influence: spiritual attitudes determine economic behaviors; then economic situations in turn retroactively influence religious and moral ways of seeing the world. In the building of the economic power Europe—after the initial movement, which had a more ethical and religious orientation—the determining factor was, more and more exclusively, economic interest. But now it is becoming ever more evident, nonetheless, that the building of economic structures and enterprises is accompanied by cultural decisions as well, which at the start are present in an unreflective way, so to speak, but then urgently demand explicit clarification. The big international conferences, such as those recently in Cairo and Beijing, are the expression of such a search for common criteria for action; they are something more than an airing of problems. One could describe them as a sort of council for world culture, during which common certitudes are supposed to be formulated and raised to the status of norms for the life of mankind. The politics of withholding or granting economic aid is one way of imposing such norms; in this regard the main preoccupation is with controlling world population growth and with making the methods devised for this purpose obligatory everywhere. The ancient ethical norms for the relation between the sexes, such as were in force in Africa in the form of tribal traditions and in the great Asian cultures as rules derived from the cosmic order and in the monotheistic religions according to the standard of the Ten Commandments, are being dissolved by a system of norms that, while based on complete sexual freedom, still consists fundamentally of a world-population quota and the technological means suited to that end. A similar trend can be found in the big conferences on climate change. In both cases what drives the participants to search for norms is their fear when faced with the limitations of the world's resources. In both cases it is a matter, on the one hand, of defending freedom in mankind's relation with reality, yet, on the other hand, it is a question of stemming the consequences of a limitless freedom. The third type of big international conference, the meeting of the leading economic powers in order to regulate what has become the global economy, has become the ideological battleground of the post-Communist era. While technology and the economy are still understood as vehicles for the radical freedom of mankind, their omnipresence, along with their inherent rules, is now regarded as a global dictatorship and is combated with an anarchic fury, in which the freedom to destroy is presented as an essential element of human freedom.

What does all this mean for the problem of Europe? It means that the project, which is unilaterally oriented toward the construction of an economic power, in fact automatically produces a sort of new system of values that must be tested in order to find out its ability to last and to create a future.

The European *Charter* that was recently approved could be described as an attempt to find a middle way between this new canon of values and the classical values of the European tradition. As an initial signpost it will certainly be helpful. Ambiguities at important points, nevertheless, demonstrate very clearly the problematic nature of such an attempt at mediation. A thorough-going discussion of the underlying questions cannot be avoided. That is not possible, naturally, within the framework of this talk. I would just like to state a little more precisely the problems that will have to be addressed. The fathers of European unification after the Second World War—as we have seen—took as their point of departure a fundamental compatibility between the moral heritage of Christianity and the moral heritage of the European Enlightenment. In the Enlightenment the biblical concept of God had been changed in a twofold direction under the influence of autonomous reason: God, the Creator and upholder of all, who continually sustains and guides the world, had become the one who had simply started up the universe. The concept of revelation had been abandoned. Spinoza's formula *Deus sive natura* [God or nature] could be considered under many aspects as typical of the Enlightenment vision. It still means, though, that people believed in a sort of nature that had been designed by God and in man's ability to understand that nature and also to appreciate it as a rational standard.

Marxism, on the other hand, introduced a radical break: the present world is a product of evolution without any rationality of its own; man alone must make a reasonable world emerge from the irrational raw material of reality. This vision—combined with Hegel's philosophy of history, the liberal dogma of progress, and the interpretation thereof in socio-economic terms—led to the attempt to establish a classless society, which was supposed to appear in the progress of history as the final product of the class struggle. In this way moral norms were ultimately reduced to one idea: whatever promotes the coming of that state of happiness is good; whatever is opposed to it is bad.

Today we find ourselves in the midst of a second Enlightenment, which has not only left behind the motto *Deus sive natura* but has also unmasked as irrational the Marxist ideology of hope. In its place it has proposed a rational goal for the future, which is entitled the New World Order and is now supposed to become in its turn the essential ethical norm. It still shares with Marxism the evolutionary idea of a universe brought forth

by an irrational event and formed by its intrinsic rules,
which however—unlike the provisions of the ancient
idea of nature—cannot contain within themselves any
ethical direction. The attempt to derive from the rules of
the evolutionary game the rules for the game of human
life as well, and hence a sort of new ethics, is in reality
rather widespread but not very convincing. There are
more and more voices of philosophers such as Singer,
Rorty, and Sloterdijk telling us that man now has the
right and the duty to construct a new world on a rational
basis. The New World Order, the necessity of which
cannot be doubted, they say, ought to be a world order of
rationality. Thus far they are all in agreement. But what
is rational? The criterion of rationality is drawn exclusively from experiences of technological production on
scientific foundations. Such rationality exists in the sense
of functionality, efficiency, increase in the quality of
life. The exploitation of nature that is connected with it
increasingly becomes a problem because of environmen-
tal hazards, which are becoming dramatic.

Meanwhile, the manipulation of man by man is
proceeding apace with even greater impudence. The
visions of Huxley are definitely becoming a reality:
the human being must be no longer begotten irratio-
nally but rather produced rationally. But man as a product is at the disposal of man. The imperfect specimens
are discarded, so as to develop the perfect man by way
of planning and production. Suffering must disappear;
life must be nothing but pleasant. Such radical visions

are still isolated instances, for the most part attenuated in many ways, but more and more often the principle of behavior is affirmed that states that it is permissible for man to do everything he is capable of doing. Possibility as such becomes a criterion that is sufficient unto itself. In a world that is understood in an evolutionary way, it is also selfevident that there cannot be any absolute values, things that are always bad or things that are always good; instead, the weighing of goods is the only way to discern moral norms. This, however, means that higher purposes, for example, presumed experimental results for the cure of diseases, justify even the exploitation of man, provided that the anticipated good appears sufficiently great.

But in this way new forms of oppression are born, and a new ruling class arises. Ultimately the destiny of other men is decided by those who have scientific power at their disposal and those who manage the finances. Not remaining behind in research becomes an obligation from which there is no escape and which itself determines the direction of it. What advice can be given to Europe and the world in this situation? A specifically European feature in this situation today appears to be precisely the separation from all ethical traditions and the exclusive reliance on technological reasoning and its possibilities. But will not a world order with these foundations become in reality a horrific utopia? Does not Europe perhaps need, does not the world perhaps need precisely some corrective elements derived from its great tradition and from the great ethical traditions of mankind? The inviolable nature of human dignity ought to become the fundamental, untouchable pillar of ethical regulations. Only if man recognizes that he is an end [and not a means], only if the human being is sacred and inviolable, can we have confidence in one another and live together in peace. There is no weighing of goods that can justify treating man as experimental material for higher ends. Only if we see here something absolute, situated above all attempts to weigh goods, do we act in a truly ethical manner and not by means of calculations. The inviolability of human dignity means also that this dignity is valid for everyone, that it has a human face and belongs biologically to the human race. Criteria of functionality cannot have any validity here. Even the human being who is suffering, disabled, or not yet born is a human being. I would like to add that this must be joined also to respect for the origin of the human being from the communion of a man and a woman. The human being cannot become a product. He cannot be produced; he can only be begotten. And for this reason protection for the special dignity of the communion between man and woman, on which the future of mankind is based, must be numbered among the ethical constants of every human society. But all this is possible only if we acquire also a new sense of the dignity of suffering. Learning to live also means learning to suffer. Therefore respect for the sacred is demanded, too. Faith in God the Creator is the surest guarantee of man's dignity. It cannot be imposed on anyone; but since it is a great good for the community, it can make the claim to respect on the part of nonbelievers. It is true: rationality is an essential hallmark of European culture. With it, from a certain perspective, it has conquered the world, because the form of rationality developed first of all in Europe informs the life of every continent today. Yet this rationality can become devastating if it becomes detached from its roots and exalts technological feasibility as the sole criterion. The bond between the two great sources of knowledge—nature and history—is necessary. These two areas do not simply speak on their own, but the two together can provide some indication of what path to take. The exploitation of nature, which rebels against an indiscriminate use, has prompted new reflections on the signposts provided by nature itself. Having dominion over nature, in the sense of the biblical story of creation, does not mean the violent utilization of nature but rather the understanding of its intrinsic possibilities, and thus it requires that careful form of utilization in which man places himself at the service of nature and nature at the service of man. The very origin of man is a process that is both natural and human: in the relation between a man and a woman the natural element and the spiritual element are united in what is specifically human, which cannot be despised without causing harm. And so the historical experiences of man, too, which are reflected in the great religions, are permanent sources of knowledge, of directions provided by reason, which are of interest even to someone who cannot identify with any of these traditions. To deliberate while bracketing them off and to live without taking them into consideration would be a presumption that would ultimately leave man disoriented and empty.

All this gives no conclusive answer to the question about the foundations of Europe. We simply wanted to sketch the contours of the task that lies ahead. It is urgent that we get to work.

PART TWO

POLITICS AND MORALITY

Political Visions and the Praxis of Politics

For politicians of all parties the obvious thing to do today is to promise changes—of course, changes for the better. Whereas currently the once legendary success of the word revolution is on the decline, definite and far-reaching reforms are being demanded and promised all the more. One would have to conclude, however, that in modern society a deep sense of dissatisfaction predominates, and this precisely in places where well-being and freedom have reached a level heretofore unknown. The world is perceived as hard to endure; it must improve, and bringing this about seems to be the task of politics. Since, therefore, according to popular opinion, improving the world, the building of a new world, constitutes the essential duty of politics, it is understandable also why the word "conservative" has become suspect and why it is unlikely that someone would want to be considered a conservative: it seems that it is a matter, not of preserving the status quo, but of surpassing it.

Two visions of the function of politics: conserving or transforming the world order

With this basic orientation, the modern concept of politics, and hence of life in this world, is situated in stark contrast to the visions of earlier periods, in which the great task of political action was deemed to be precisely the preservation and the defense of existing conditions against threats to them. Here a minor linguistic note can help clarify things. When Christianity was looking in the Roman world for a word with which it could express, in a synthetic way understandable to everyone, what Jesus Christ meant to them, it came across the word *conservator*, which had designated in Rome the essential duty and the highest service necessary to render to mankind. But this very title the Christians could not and would not transfer to their Redeemer; with that term, indeed, they could not translate the word Messiah or Christ or describe the task of the Savior of the world. From the perspective of the Roman Empire, indeed, it would necessarily seem that the most important duty was that of preserving the situation of the empire against all internal and external threats, since this empire embodied a period of peace and justice in which men could live in security and dignity. In fact Christians—even during the apostolic age—were able to appreciate this safeguard of justice and peace that the Roman Empire offered. The Fathers of the Church, who were faced with menacing chaos at the onset of invasions by other peoples, were certainly interested in maintaining the empire and its legal guarantees, its peaceful social order. Nevertheless, Christians could not simply want everything to remain as it was; the Book of Revelation, which with its vision of the empire is no doubt situated at an extreme position in the New Testament, clearly demonstrated to all that there was also something that could not be preserved but had to be changed. The fact that Christ could be described, not as *Conservator*, but as *Salvator* certainly had no political or revolutionary significance, but it nevertheless indicated the limits of mere conservatism and pointed to a dimension of human life that goes beyond the causes of peace and order, which are the proper subject of politics.

Let us look a little more closely at this particular instance of a form of existential understanding of the task of politics. Behind the alternative that has just been shown to us rather indistinctly in the contrast between the titles *Conservator* and *Salvator* are in reality two visions of what political and ethical action can and should accomplish, in which not only politics and morality, but also politics, religion, and morality appear to be mutually intertwined in various ways. On the one hand, there is the static vision, oriented toward conservation, that perhaps is manifested most evidently in Chinese universalism: the order of heaven, eternally the same, offers its standard for earthly action as well. This is the Tao, the law of being and of reality, which men must acknowledge and take up again in their action. The Tao is both a cosmic and a moral law. It safeguards the harmony of heaven and earth, and thus it is also the harmony of political and social life. Disorder, disturbance of the peace, and chaos arise when man turns against the Tao and lives without regard for it or in a way contrary to it. Then, in compensation for such disturbances and havoc in common life, the Tao must be restored, and thus the world is once again made livable. Everything depends on the preservation of the lasting order or on the return to it, whenever it has been abandoned. Something analogous is expressed in the Indian concept of Dharma, which means the cosmic order that is also ethical and social, to which man must conform so that life will unfold harmoniously. Buddhism has relativized this simultaneously cosmic, political, and religious vision, inasmuch as it has viewed the whole world as a cycle of suffering; salvation is sought, not in the cosmos, but in departing from it. But Buddhism created no new political vision, inasmuch as the search for salvation is understood in an unworldly way, as directed toward Nirvana; for the world as such no new models are proposed.

The faith of Israel is different. Granted, with the strict covenant between God and Noah, it, too, knows something like a cosmic order and the promise of its stability. But for the faith of Israel itself, the orientation toward the future becomes increasingly evident. Salvation is located, not in what is eternally motionless, not in a today that is always the same, but rather in tomorrow, in the future that is not yet present. The Book of

Daniel, which was composed during the second century before Christ, presents two grand historical-theological visions, which became tremendously important for the later development of political and religious thought. In the second chapter we read about the vision of the statue, which is made up partly of gold, partly of silver, partly of iron, and lastly of clay as well. These four materials signify a succession of four kingdoms. Finally, all of them are destroyed by a stone that is cut from a mountain without the work of human hands and that reduces the whole statue to dust, so that the wind carries the debris away and not a trace of it remains. The stone, however, becomes a great mountain and fills the whole earth—the symbol of a kingdom set up by the God of heaven and earth that will never decline for all eternity (2:44). The seventh chapter of the same book presents the series of kingdoms with perhaps even more impressive symbolism as a succession of four beasts, on which God—described as "the Ancient of Days"— passes judgment at last. The four beasts—the great empires of world history—had come out of the sea, which symbolically represents the mighty threat to life posed by death and its powers; after the Judgment, however, one like a man ("a son of man") arrives from heaven, and to him are given all peoples, nations, and languages through an eternal kingdom that will never be destroyed and will never pass away.

In the concepts of Tao and Dharma, the eternal decrees of the cosmos play such an important role that the idea of "history" does not appear at all, whereas here "history" is understood as a specific reality that cannot be reduced to the cosmos, and with this previously unnoticed anthropological and dynamic reality is inaugurated a completely different vision. It is clear that this depiction of the historical succession of kingdoms as monstrous, voracious beasts, one more terrible than the other, could not have developed in one of the ruling peoples; rather, it presupposes as its sociological basis a people that is conscious of being threatened by the voracity of these beasts and has also experienced a succession of powers that have challenged its right to exist. It is the vision of the oppressed, who are looking forward to a turn of historical events and have no interest in preserving the status quo. In Daniel's vision, the turning point in history does not arrive through political or military action—the forces necessary for that are simply not there. The change comes about solely through a divine intervention: the stone that destroys the kingdoms is cut from a mountain "by no human hand" (2:34). The Fathers of the Church saw in this a mysterious foretelling of the birth of Jesus from the Virgin, solely by the power of God; in Christ they see the stone that finally becomes a mountain and fills the earth. What is new with respect to the cosmic visions in which Tao or Dharma itself is presented as the divine power or as the "divine" is therefore not only the appearance of history that cannot be reduced to the cosmos, but also this third reality that is at the same time the first: a

God who acts, to whom the oppressed turn their hopes. But already at the time of the Maccabees, who date from about the same period as Daniel's visions, man, too, must take up God's cause by political and military action; in some parts of the Qumran literature the fusion of theological hope with what is properly human action becomes even more evident. Finally, the battle of Bar Kocheba indicates a clear politicization of messianism: in order to bring about a change, God makes use of a "Messiah", whom God commissions and authorizes to introduce the new thing by means of political and military action.

The *sacrum imperium* of the Christians, in its Byzantine as well as its Latin variations, was neither able nor willing to adopt such concepts, especially since it was newly engaged in preserving the world order that now had a Christian foundation. Besides, it was convinced that it was in the sixth age of history, in the period of old age, after which would come the next world, which as God's eighth day was already running parallel with history and would therefore succeed it forever.

The rebirth of the apocalyptic trend in the twentieth century

The apocalyptic trend—that is, the No to the prevailing forces in the world and the hope of turning back and thus of saving the world—emerges in a new way, now a-religious and often anti-religious, beginning with the eighteenth century. Its radical form is found in Marxism, which joins Daniel in assigning a negative value to all of preceding history as a story of oppression and, furthermore, in assuming that it has sociological support from the exploited class, first of all from workers who are deprived of all rights and also from tenant farmers. In a surprising reversal, the reasons for which have not yet been studied sufficiently, Marxism then increasingly became in the West the religion of the intellectuals, whereas workers had won their rights through reforms, which made it superfluous for them to plan the revolution—the great escape from the historical status quo. As a result of reforms in the social system, they no longer needed the stone that destroyed the kingdoms: they were betting instead on the other figure from Daniel—the lion, who stood up on two feet like a man and to whom was given the heart of a man (cf. 7:4). Reform replaces revolution: if the lion has a human heart, it is possible to live with the lion.

In the world of the intellectuals—who were often very well-to-do—what developed instead was the forceful No to "reformism", a quasi-apotheosis of revolution. In their view, an entirely new world had to be created: one observes in them a weariness with the real world, the causes for which have not been analyzed sufficiently. But let us try now to understand the structure and the intellectual components of this new type of apocalypse. The foundation of this concept of history consists, on the one hand, in the theory of evolution transferred to

history, and, on the other hand—not entirely uncon-
nected with the previous element—in Hegel's version
of faith in progress. The connection with the theory of
evolution means that history is seen in a biologistic, that
is, materialistic and deterministic mode: it has its laws
and runs its course, against which one can struggle but
which cannot be stopped after all. God is replaced with
evolution. Now "God" means development, progress. But this progress—and here Hegel comes in—is
accomplished in dialectical movements; it, too, is ultimately understood in a deterministic form. The final
dialectical stage is the leap from the history of oppression into the definitive history of salvation—the passage
from the beasts to the Son of Man, one could say along
with Daniel. The reign of the Son of Man is now called
"the classless society". Although from one perspective
the dialectical leaps occur necessarily as natural events
according to this philosophy, concretely speaking they
in fact come about—as some see it—by way of political action. The political equivalent of the dialectical
leap is revolution. This is the opposite of reform, which
must be rejected, because it actually gives the impression that the heart of a man has been given to the beast
and that it is no longer necessary to fight it. Reforms—
so they say—destroy the revolutionary impulse; therefore they are opposed to the internal logic of history;
they are an involution instead of an evolution, and
hence, when all is said and done, they are inimical to
progress. Revolution and utopia—the nostalgia for a

perfect world—are connected: they are the concrete form of this new political, secularized messianism. The idol of the future devours the present; the idol of revolution is the adversary of reasonable political action aimed at making concrete improvements to the world. The theological vision of Daniel, and of apocalyptic literature in general, is applied to secular reality, but at the same time it is mythologized and profoundly distorted. Indeed, the two foundational political ideas—revolution and utopia—are, in connection with evolution and the dialectic, an absolutely anti-rational myth: it is urgently necessary to demythologize them, so that politics can carry on its work in a truly reasonable way.

The position of the New Testament Scriptures

But apart from Daniel and political messianism, where does the Christian faith stand on these issues? What is its vision of history, and how much importance does it assign to our historical action? Before I can attempt to formulate an overall judgment, we must take a look at the most important passages in the New Testament. Here, without elaborate analyses, we can easily distinguish two groups of texts: on the one hand, there are passages from the Gospels and the Acts of the Apostles that offer a glimpse of distant connections with apocalyptic literature; on the other hand, there is the Apocalypse of John, which, as the very title suggests, belongs to the apocalyptic genre. It is well known that the passages from the letters written by the apostles, in keeping with the vision outlined in the Gospels, show no signs whatsoever of revolutionary fervor; on the contrary, they are clearly opposed to revolution. The two fundamental texts, Romans 13:1–6 and 1 Peter 2:13–17, are very clear and have always been a thorn in the side for revolutionaries. Romans 13 demands that "every person" (literally: every soul) be subject to the governing authorities, because there is no authority unless God gives it. Opposition to authority is therefore opposition to the order established by God. Hence one should submit not only by constraint, but by reason of conscience. In quite similar terms the First Letter of Peter requires submission to the lawful authorities "for the Lord's sake": "For it is God's will that by doing right you should put to silence the ignorance of foolish men. Live as free men, yet without using your freedom as a pretext for evil. . . ." Neither Paul nor Peter is glorifying the Roman State uncritically. Although they affirm the divine origin of the State's legal ordinances, they are very far from divinizing the State. Precisely because they see the limits of the State, which is not God and cannot be presented as God, they recognize the purpose of its ordinances and its moral value. Thus they take their place in a good biblical tradition—think of Jeremiah, who exhorts the exiled Israelites to fidelity in their confrontation with the oppressive State of Babylon, inasmuch as this State guarantees law and order and thus also the relative welfare of Israel, which is the prerequisite for its restoration as a people. Think of Deutero-Isaiah, who does not hesitate to call Cyrus the anointed one of God: the king of the Persians, who does not know the God of Israel and makes the people return to their homeland out of purely pragmatic political considerations, nonetheless acts as God's instrument from the moment he pledges to reestablish the Law. Along these lines also is Jesus' response to the Pharisees and the Herodians with regard to their question about taxes: what is Caesar's must be given to Caesar (Mk 12:13–17). To the extent that the Roman emperor safeguards the law, he can demand obedience. Of course, the scope of the duty of obedience is reduced at the same time: there are the things that are Caesar's and those that are God's. Whenever Caesar exalts himself as God, he has exceeded his limits, and obedience then would be the denial of God. Essentially along these same lines is Jesus' reply to Pilate, in which the Lord, in the presence of an unjust judge, still acknowledges that the authority to act as judge, a role of service to the law, can be given only from above (Jn 19:11).

If we consider these correlations, a very moderate concept of the State appears. The crucial thing is not the personal credibility or the subjective good intentions of the organs of the State. In the measure that they safeguard peace and uphold the law, they correspond to a divine decree. In today's terminology, we might say that they represent a creaturely arrangement. The State is to be respected precisely in its secularity. The necessary starting point is man's nature as a *social and political animal*;

the State is founded on this human nature and thus corresponds with the plan of creation. All of this involves at the same time a limitation of the State; it has its sphere, which it cannot surpass; it must respect the higher law of God. The refusal to adore the emperor and in general the refusal to worship the State is at bottom simply the refusal of the totalitarian State. In the First Letter of Peter this line of demarcation is clearly evident when the Apostle says, "But let none of you suffer as a murderer, or a thief, or a wrongdoer, or a mischief-maker; yet if one suffers as a Christian, let him not be ashamed, but under that name let him glorify God" (4:15f.). The Christian is bound by the juridical order of the State as though by a moral precept. It is something different when he suffers "as a Christian": when the State punishes Christianity as such, it is exercising its power, not as a guarantor, but rather as a destroyer of the law. Then it is not shameful but an honor to be punished. Anyone who suffers for this reason becomes precisely in his suffering a follower of Christ: the crucified Christ indicates the limits of State power and shows where its laws come to an end and resistance through suffering becomes necessary. The faith of the New Testament does not know of the revolutionary but is acquainted with the martyr: the martyr recognizes the authority of the State but also knows its limits. His resistance consists in the fact that he does everything that serves the law and the organized community, even if it comes from an authority that is a stranger to the faith or hostile to it, but he does not obey when he is ordered to do evil, that is, to go against the will of God. His resistance is not the active resistance of violence but rather the resistance of one who is ready to suffer for the will of God. The combatant in a resistance movement who dies with a weapon in hand is not a martyr in the New Testament sense.

We find the same line of thinking even if we look at other New Testament passages that take positions in confronting the problem of Christian conduct with respect to the State. Titus 3:1 says, "Remind them to be submissive to rulers and authorities, to be obedient, to be ready for any honest work." Another very revealing passage is 2 Thessalonians 3:10–12, in which the Apostle addresses the situation of those who—no doubt under the pretext that as Christians they are awaiting the Lord's return—do not work and do not want to do anything useful. He admonishes them to work quietly instead, because "if any one will not work, let him not eat." An over-enthusiastic eschatology is forcefully summoned to reconsider its priorities. An important aspect appears also in 1 Timothy 2:2, where Christians are exhorted to pray for the king and all authorities, "that we may lead a quiet and peaceable life". Two things are clearly apparent here: Christians pray for the king and the authorities, but they do not adore the king. The letter is either from the time of Nero—if Paul is the author of it—or, if a later date is assigned to it, from around the time of Domitian; both were tyrants hostile to Christianity. Nevertheless, Christians pray for the one who governs, that he might be able to carry out his duties. Of course, whenever he makes himself God, they refuse him obedience. The second element consists in the fact that the duty of the State is formulated in extraordinarily moderate terms that seem almost trivial: it should be concerned about peace at home and with its neighbors. As we have said, this may sound rather commonplace, but in reality it expresses an essentially moral standard: internal and external peace are possible only when the essential rights of man and of the community are respected and guaranteed.

Now let us attempt to incorporate these findings into the perspectives we examined previously. It seems to me that two things could be said. The dynamic historical vision associated with the apocalyptic and messianic hopes makes its appearance only indirectly; messianism is essentially transformed by the figure of Jesus. It remains politically relevant insofar as it indicates the point at which martyrdom becomes necessary, thus defining precisely the limit of the State's rights. Every martyr, however, is secure in the promise of the risen Christ who will come again; in this sense, he points beyond the present world to a new, definitive communion of men with God and with one another. But this limitation of the scope of the State and this opening of the horizon to a new world in the future do not abolish current state regulations, which, being based on natural reason and logic, should continue to govern and are valid regulations for historical time. An enthusiastic

eschatological-revolutionary messianism is absolutely
foreign to the New Testament. History is, so to speak,
the kingdom of reason; politics does not establish the
Kingdom of God, but it certainly ought to be concerned about the just kingdom of man, which means
to create the conditions for domestic and international
peace and for a kind of justice in which all "may lead a
quiet and peaceable life, godly and respectful in every
way" (1 Tim 2:2). It could be said that the New Testament passages also express the postulate of religious liberty while considering reason to be capable of knowing
the essential moral foundations of the human being and
to put them into effect politically. In this sense, there is
at least a distant relationship to the positions proposed
by Tao or Dharma as the basis for the State. Therefore
Christians were able to take a positive view of the Stoic
idea of the natural moral law, which proposed analogous concepts within the context of Greek philosophy.
The notion that history has its own dynamic, a belief
that is particularly evident in the Book of Daniel (which
does not consider history simply in a cosmic manner
but interprets it as a forward-moving dynamic of good
and evil), remains present through messianic hope. This
makes clear the moral criteria for politics and indicates
the limits of political power, thanks to the horizon of
hope, which allows us to glimpse what is beyond history and gives us the courage to act rightly and to suffer
well within it. In this sense, one can speak of a synthesis of the cosmic and historical visions. I believe that,

starting from here, one can also define exactly where the boundary runs between the Christian apocalyptic vision and the non-Christian, Gnostic variety. An apocalyptic vision is Christian when it maintains the connection with faith in creation; wherever faith in creation, its permanence, and its reliance on reason are abandoned, one steps from Christian faith over into Gnosticism. Within these fundamental options there are no doubt many possible variations, but it is certain that they all proceed from one basic alternative. An analysis of the passages, which is not possible here, could demonstrate that the Apocalypse of John, however much its spirit of resistance distinguishes it from apostolic writings, remains very clearly within the parameters of the Christian option.

Consequences for the political involvement of the Christian today

What can be concluded from all this in regard to the relation between political vision and political practice today? On this subject there should be a very thorough discussion, which I do not feel competent to conduct. Nevertheless, I would like to present briefly, in the form of two theses, several notes on how these elements can be applied to today.

1. Politics is the sphere of reason; more precisely, not a purely technical, calculating reason, but moral reasoning,

since the end of the State, and thus the ultimate purpose
of all politics, is by its very nature moral, namely, peace
and justice. This means that moral reasoning about, or
more precisely, rational discernment of what fosters justice and peace (and therefore is moral) must be constantly carried on and defended against all that could
obscure and diminish reason's capacity for discernment.
The party mentality that goes along with power will
always produce myths in various forms, which are presented as the true path of moral reality in politics but are
in fact merely masks and disguises of power. In the past
century we experienced two myths that were worked
out on a grandiose scale with terrible consequences:
racism, with its false promise of salvation on the part
of National Socialism, and the apotheosis of revolution
against the background of historical-dialectical evolu-
tionism. In both cases the original moral intuitions of
man concerning good and evil were in effect abolished.
Everything that promoted the rule of the race, or else
everything that promoted the establishment of the future
world, is good—so it was said—even something that
would have been an evil according to the consciousness
that mankind had previously attained.

     After the fall of the grand ideologies, political myths
today are presented in less obvious ways, but mythologized forms of real values still exist, which appear credible precisely because they are anchored to authentic
values, but for this very reason they are also dangerous,
in that they oversimplify these values in a way that can be

described as mythical. I would say that nowadays three values are predominant in the general consciousness, yet their mythical oversimplification at the same time poses a threat to moral reasoning today. These three values that are constantly, mythically oversimplified are: progress, science, and freedom.

Progress has always been a mythical word, which is imposed as a norm for political and human action in general and appears to be its highest moral qualification. Anyone looking back at the course of the last hundred years alone cannot deny that enormous progress has been made in medicine, in technology, in understanding and exploiting the forces of nature, and there is hope for still further progress. Nevertheless, the ambivalence of this progress still remains a cause for concern. Progress is becoming a menace to creation, the very basis for our existence. It produces inequalities among men and, furthermore, continually produces new threats to the world and to mankind. In this sense it is absolutely necessary to guide progress according to moral criteria. But what criteria? That is the problem. Above all it must be made clear that the scope of progress extends as far as the relations of man with the material world, but progress as such does not give rise to a new man, to a new society, as Marxism and liberalism taught. Man *qua* man remains the same in primitive conditions as in technologically developed societies and does not advance to a higher level simply by the fact that he has learned to employ more highly developed tools. Human nature starts over from the beginning in every human being. Therefore there cannot be such a thing as a definitively new, advanced, and smooth-running society. Not only was this the hope of the grand ideologies, but it has been becoming more and more the general objective expected by all ever since hope in the hereafter was demolished. A definitively well-run society would presuppose the end of freedom. However, because man always remains free, it starts over with each generation; therefore, one must always work for a just form of society under ever-new conditions. The field of politics, however, is the present and not the future—it concerns the future only to the extent that contemporary politics seeks to create forms of law and peace that can be valid tomorrow as well and attempts to encourage appropriate reforms that reaffirm and continue what has been achieved. But we cannot guarantee it. I think that it is very important to keep in mind these limits of progress and to avoid escapist and deceptive prospects for the future.

In the second place, I would like to mention the concept of science. Science is a great good, precisely because it is a form of rationality that is tested and confirmed by experience. But there are also pathological forms of science, distortions of its possibilities for the sake of power, whereby at the same time human dignity is attacked. Science can also be put at the service of man's inhumanity to man: think of weapons of mass destruction or experiments on human beings or trafficking in human organs for transplantation, and so on.

Therefore it must be perfectly clear that science, too, must be subject to moral criteria and that its true nature is always lost whenever, instead of serving the dignity of man, it is placed at the disposal of power or of commerce or it takes simple success as its sole criterion.

Finally there is the concept of freedom. It, too, has assumed various mythical traits in the modern era. Not infrequently freedom is understood in an anarchic and simply anti-institutional manner and thus becomes an idol. Authentic human freedom can only be the freedom of just reciprocal relations, the freedom of justice; otherwise it becomes a lie and leads to slavery.

2. The purpose of all necessary demythologizing is to restore reason to its proper place and function. Here, however, we must once again unmask a myth that confronts us with the ultimate and decisive question for a politics of reason: the myth that a majority decision in many or, perhaps, in most cases is the "most reasonable" way to arrive at a solution for everyone. But the majority cannot be the ultimate principle; there are values that no majority has the right to repeal. The killing of the innocent can never become a right and cannot be raised to the status of a right by any authority.

Here, too, we are dealing ultimately with the defense of reason: reason, moral reasoning, is superior to the majority. But how can we know these ultimate values that constitute the foundations of all "reasonable", morally just politics and therefore bind everyone, regardless of all shifting majorities? What are these values? The philosophical doctrine about the State, in antiquity and in the Middle Ages and even in the debates of the modern era, has appealed to the natural law, which *recta ratio* [right reason] can recognize. But today this *recta ratio* no longer seems to provide an answer, and natural law is regarded, not as something self-evident to all, but rather as a specifically Catholic doctrine. This means a crisis of political reasoning, which is tantamount to a crisis of politics as such. Now, it seems, there is only partisan reasoning, instead of reason that is common to all men, at least in major, fundamental value judgments. Working to overcome this situation is an urgent task for all those who have responsibility for peace and justice in the world—and that definitely means all of us. Indeed, there are prospects for success in this task, precisely because reason continually asserts itself against power and the partisan spirit.

Nowadays there is a canon of changed values that in practice is not called into question, even though in reality it is still too indefinite and has its gray areas. The triad of peace, justice, and respect for the environment is universally recognized but completely indeterminate with regard to its contents. What promotes peace? What is justice? What is the best way to protect the environment? Other universally recognized values are: the equality of men (as opposed to racism), the equal dignity of the sexes, freedom of thought, and freedom of religion. Here, too, there are ambiguities with regard to the contents of these concepts, which again can even become threats to freedom of thought and freedom of religion, but the basic orientations are valid and important. One essential point remains controversial: the right to life for every human being, the inviolability of human life at every stage. In the name of freedom and in the name of science, increasingly serious wounds are being inflicted with regard to this right. Whenever abortion is considered a right, a personal freedom, the freedom of one person is placed above the right to life of another. When experiments on human embryos are justified in the name of science, the dignity of the human being is denied and trampled on in the case of the most defenseless. Here we must work to demythologize the concepts of freedom and science if we do not want to lose the foundations for all rights, along with respect for man and his dignity.

A second gray area is the freedom to ridicule what is sacred to others. Thank God, in our society no one is allowed to make fun of what is sacred to a Jew or a Muslim. Yet numbered among the fundamental rights and freedoms is the right to mock and cover with ridicule the things that Christians hold sacred.

And finally there is one last gray area: marriage and family no longer seem to be fundamental values of a modern society. In the present situation, therefore, completing the table of values and demythologizing the values that have been altered mythically are urgent priorities.

In my debate with the philosopher Flores d'Arcais we touched on just this point: the limits of the principle of consensus. The philosopher could not deny that there are values that cannot be called into question, even by majorities. But which ones? Faced with this question, the moderator of the debate, Gad Lerner, posed the question: Why not take the Ten Commandments as the standard? And in fact, the Decalogue is not the private property of Christians or Jews. It is an exalted expression of moral reasoning that, as such, is largely in agreement with the wisdom of the other major cultures. Referring again to the Ten Commandments could be essential precisely for the restoration of reason, for a new launching of *recta ratio*.

Here it becomes quite clear what faith can do to promote good politics: it does not replace reason, but it can help to make essential values more evident. Faith that is lived out concretely confers upon these values a credibility that then enlightens and heals reason as well. In the century that has just been completed, as in all centuries, it was precisely the testimony of the martyrs that set limits to the excesses of power and thus contributed decisively to the restoration of sound reason.

2

That Which Holds the World Together: The Prepolitical Moral Foundations of a Free State

Historical developments are moving more and more quickly in today's world, and I believe that two factors in particular typify this acceleration of a process that began only slowly in the past. *First*, we have the formation of a global community in which the individual political,

The Catholic Academy of Bavaria, with headquarters in Munich, sponsored an evening forum on January 19, 2004, in which Professor Jürgen Habermas, the most renowned exponent of the secular vision of the State, and I, as a representative of the classical Catholic tradition, had to present in brief talks our respective visions of the moral foundations of the State. Participating in the forum was a select audience made up of philosophers, political scientists, and theologians who were invited to discuss the talks and the topic itself together with the speakers. Since then the two talks have been published several times. Nevertheless, because the questions addressed at that forum are quite closely connected with the issues discussed in this little volume, the text is reprinted here.

This chapter was translated by Brian McNeil, C.R.V., and also published in *Dialectics of Secularization: On Reason and Religion*, by Joseph Cardinal Ratzinger and Jürgen Habermas (San Francisco: Ignatius Press, 2006).

economic, and cultural powers become increasingly dependent on one another, touching and intersecting each other in their various existential spheres. *Secondly*, we have the development of human possibilities, of the power to make and to destroy, that poses the question of legal and ethical controls on power in a way that goes far beyond anything to which we have yet been accustomed. This lends great urgency to the question of how cultures that encounter one another can find ethical bases to guide their relationship along the right path, thus permitting them to build up a common structure that tames power and imposes a legally responsible order on the exercise of power.

The fact that Hans Küng's proposal of a "world ethos" interests so many people shows at any rate that this question has in fact been posed; and this remains a valid point, even if one agrees with Robert Spaemann's acute critique of this project.[1] This is because we must add a third factor to the two mentioned above. In the process of encounter and mutual penetration of cultures, ethical certainties that had hitherto provided solid foundations have largely disintegrated. The question of what the good is (especially in the given context of our world) and of why one must do the good even when this entails harm to one's own self—this fundamental question goes generally unanswered.

---

[1] R. Spaemann, "Weltethos als 'Projekt'", *Merkur*, no. 570/571 (1996): 893–904.

It seems to me obvious that science as such cannot give birth to such an ethos. In other words, a renewed ethical consciousness does not come about as the product of academic debates. On the other hand, it is equally indisputable that the fundamental transformation of the understanding of the world and of man that has come about thanks to the growth in scientific knowledge has played a major role in the collapse of the old moral certainties. And this means that science does have a responsibility vis-à-vis man *qua* man. In particular, it is the responsibility of philosophy to accompany critically the development of the individual academic disciplines, shedding a critical light on premature conclusions and apparent "certainties" about what man is, whence he comes, and what the goal of his existence is. To make the same point in different words: philosophy must sift the non-scientific element out of the scientific results with which it is often entangled, thus keeping open our awareness of the totality and of the broader dimensions of the reality of human existence—for science can never show us more than partial aspects of this existence.

1. Power and law

It is the specific task of politics to apply the criterion of the law to power, thereby structuring the use of power in a meaningful manner. It is not the law of the stronger, but the strength of the law that must hold sway. Power as structured by law, and at the service of the law, is the antithesis of violence, which is a lawless power that opposes the law. This is why it is important for every society to overcome any suspicion that is cast on the law and its regulations, for it is only in this way that arbitrariness can be excluded and freedom can be experienced as a freedom shared in common with others. Freedom without law is anarchy and, hence, the destruction of freedom. Suspicion of the law, revolt against the law, will always arise when law itself appears to be no longer the expression of a justice that is at the service of all but rather the product of arbitrariness and legislative arrogance on the part of those who have power.

This is why the task of applying the criterion of the law to power leads to a further question: How does law come into being, and what must be the characteristics of law if it is to be the vehicle of justice rather than the privilege of those who have the power to make the law? It is, on the one hand, the question of the genesis of the law, but, on the other hand, the question of its own inherent criteria. The problem that law must be, not the instrument of the power of a few, but the expression of the common interest of all, seems—at first sight—to have been resolved through the instruments whereby a democratic will is formed in society, since all collaborate in the genesis of the law. This means that it is everyone's law; it can and must be respected, precisely because it is everyone's law. And as a sheer matter of fact, the guarantee of a shared collaboration in the elaboration of the

law and in the just administration of power is the basic
argument that speaks in favor of democracy as the most
appropriate form of political order. And yet it seems to me that one question remains
unanswered. Since total consensus among men is very
hard to achieve, the process of forming a democratic
will relies necessarily either on an act of delegation or
else on a majority decision; depending on the importance of the question at issue, the proportion of the
majority that is required may differ. But majorities, too,
can be blind or unjust, as history teaches us very plainly.
When a majority (even if it is an utterly preponderant
majority) oppresses a religious or a racial minority by
means of unjust laws, can we still speak in this instance
of justice or, indeed, of law? In other words, the majority principle always leaves open the question of the
ethical foundations of the law. This is the question of
whether there is something that can never become law
but always remains injustice; or, to reverse this formu-
lation, whether there is something that is of its very
nature inalienably law, something that is antecedent to
every majority decision and must be respected by all
such decisions.

The modern period has formulated a number of
such normative elements in the various declarations
of human rights and has withdrawn these from subjection to the vagaries of majorities. It is of course possible for the contemporary consciousness to be content
with the inherent obviousness of these values. But even

such a self-limitation of the act of questioning has a philosophical character! There are then, let us say, self-subsistent values that flow from the essence of what it is to be a man, and are therefore inviolable: no other man can infringe them. We will have to return later to the question of the extent to which this idea can be sustained, above all because the obviousness of these values is by no means acknowledged in every culture. Islam has defined its own catalogue of human rights, which differs from the Western catalogue. And if my information is correct, although it is true that today's China is defined by a cultural form, namely Marxism, that arose in the West, it is asking whether "human rights" are merely a typically Western invention—and one that must be looked at critically.

2. New forms of power and new questions about how these are to be mastered

When we are speaking of the relationship between power and law and about the sources of law, we must also look more closely at the phenomenon of power itself. I do not propose to try to define the essence of "power" as such. Instead, I should like to sketch the challenges that emerge from the new forms of power that have developed in the last fifty years.

The first phase of the period after the Second World War was dominated by fear of the new destructive power that the invention of the atomic bomb had placed in the hands of men. Man suddenly realized that he was capable of destroying both himself and his planet. This prompted the question: What political mechanisms are necessary in order to prevent this destruction? How can such mechanisms be discovered and made effective? How can we mobilize the ethical energies that give birth to political forms of this kind and make them work? Then, for a long period, it was the competition between the opposing power blocs, and the fear that the destruction of the other side would lead to one's own destruction, that preserved us de facto from the terrors of a nuclear war. The mutual limitation of power and the fear for one's own survival proved powerful enough to save the world.

By now, however, we are afraid, not so much of a largescale war, as of the omnipresent terror that can make itself felt and can strike anywhere. We now see that mankind does not need a large-scale war in order to make the world uninhabitable. The anonymous powers of terror, which can be present anywhere, are strong enough to pursue everyone into the sphere of everyday life. And all the time, there is the specter of criminal elements gaining access to weapons of mass destruction and unleashing chaos in the world, independent of the established political structures. This has shifted the question about law and ethos. We now ask what are the sources on which *terror* draws. How can we succeed in eliminating, from within, this new sickness of mankind? It is shocking to see here that, at least in part, terror offers a moral legitimation for its actions. Bin Laden's messages portray terror as the response of the powerless and oppressed peoples to the arrogance of the mighty and as the righteous punishment for their arrogance and for their blasphemous highhandedness and cruelty. Clearly, for people in certain social and political situations, such motivations are persuasive. In part, terrorist actions are portrayed as the defense of religious tradition against the godlessness of Western society.

At this point, another question arises, to which we must return later. If one of the sources of terrorism is religious fanaticism—and this is in fact the case—*is then religion a healing and saving force? Or is it not rather an archaic and dangerous force* that builds up false universalisms, thereby leading to intolerance and acts of terrorism? Must not religion, therefore, be placed under the guardianship of reason, and its boundaries carefully marked off? This, of course, prompts yet another question: Who can do this? And how does one do it? But the general question remains: Ought we to consider the gradual abolition of religion, the overcoming of religion, to be necessary progress on the part of mankind, so that it may find the path to freedom and to universal tolerance? Or is this view mistaken?

In the meantime, yet another form of power has taken center stage. At first glance, it appears to be wholly beneficial and entirely praiseworthy. In reality, however, it can become a new kind of threat to man. Man is now capable of making human beings, of producing them in test tubes (so to speak). Man becomes a product, and this entails a total alteration of man's relationship to his own self. He is no longer a gift of nature or of the Creator God; he is his own product. Man has descended into the very wellsprings of power, to the sources of his own existence. The temptation to construct the "right" man at long last, the temptation to experiment with human beings, the temptation to see them as rubbish to be discarded—all this is no mere fantasy of moralists opposed to "progress".

If we have noted the urgent question of whether religion is truly a positive force, so we must now *doubt the reliability of reason*. For in the last analysis, even the atomic bomb is a product of reason; in the last analysis, the breeding and selection of human beings is something thought up by reason. Does this then mean that it is reason that ought to be placed under guardianship? But by whom or by what? Or should perhaps religion and reason restrict each other and remind each other where their limits are, thereby encouraging a positive path? Once again, we are confronted with the question how—in a global society with its mechanisms of power and its uncontrolled forces and its varying views of what constitutes law and morality—an effective ethical conviction can be found with sufficient motivation and vigor to answer the challenges I have outlined here and to help us meet these tests.

94

3. Presuppositions of the law: Law—nature—reason

Our first step is to look at historical situations comparable
to our own, insofar as there is anything genuinely comparable. In any case, it is worth taking a very brief glance
at ancient Greece, which also experienced an Enlightenment in which a divinely based law lost its obviousness,
and it became necessary to look for deeper justifications
of the law. This led to the idea that in the face of a positive law that can in reality be injustice, there must be a
law that derives from the nature, from the very being, of
man himself. And this law must be discovered, so that it
can act as a corrective to the positive law.

Closer to our own times, we have the double rupture
of the European consciousness that occurred at the beginning of the modern period and made necessary a new fundamental reflection on both the contents and the source
of law. First, we have the exodus from the boundaries of
the European world, the Christian world, that happened
when America was discovered. Now, Europeans encoun-
tered peoples who did not belong to the Christian structures of faith and law, which had hitherto been the source
of law for everyone and which had given this structure
its form. There was no legal fellowship with these peoples. But did this mean that they were outside the law,
as some asserted at that time (and as was frequently the
case in practice)? Or is there a law that transcends all legal
systems, a law that is binding on men *qua* men in their
mutual relationships and that tells them what to do? In

this situation, Francisco de Vitoria developed the already-existing idea of the *ius gentium*, the "law of the nations"; the word *gentes* also carries the association of "pagans", "non-Christians". This designates that law which is antecedent to the Christian legal form and is charged with ordering the right relations among all peoples.

The second rupture in the Christian world took place within Christianity itself through the division in faith that led to the disintegration of the one fellowship of Christians into a number of distinct fellowships, some of which were directly hostile to each other. Once again, it was necessary to elaborate a law, or at least a legal minimum, antecedent to dogma; the sources of this law then had to lie, no longer in faith, but in nature and in human reason. Hugo Grotius, Samuel von Pufendorf, and others developed the idea of the natural law, which transcends the confessional borders of faith by establishing reason as the instrument whereby law can be posited in common.

The natural law has remained (especially in the Catholic Church) the key issue in dialogues with the secular society and with other communities of faith in order to appeal to the reason we share in common and to seek the basis for a consensus about the ethical principles of law in a secular, pluralistic society. Unfortunately, this instrument has become blunt. Accordingly, I do not intend to appeal to it for support in this conversation. The idea of the natural law presupposed a concept of nature in which nature and reason overlap, since nature itself is rational. With the victory of the theory of evolution, this view of nature has capsized: nowadays, we think that nature as such is not rational, even if there is rational behavior in nature. This is the diagnosis that is presented to us, and there seem to be few voices today that are raised to contradict it.[2] This means that, of the various dimensions of the concept of nature on which the earlier concept of the natural law was based, only one remains. Ulpian summed this up in the early third century after Christ in the well known words: "Ius naturae est, quod natura omnia animalia docet."[3] But this is not an adequate answer to our question, since we are interested, not in that which concerns all the *animalia*, but in

[2] This philosophy of evolution, which still remains dominant despite corrections on individual points, is most consistently and impressively expressed by J. Monod, *Chance and Necessity:An Essay on the Natural Philosophy of Modern Biology* (New York, 1971). On the distinction between the de facto results of the investigations of the natural sciences and the philosophy that accompanies these, R. Junker and S. Scherer, eds., *Evolution: Ein kritisches Lehrbuch*, 4th ed. (Giessen, 1998), is helpful. On the debate with the philosophy that accompanies the theory of evolution, see my *Glaube—Wahrheit—Toleranz* (Freiburg im Breisgau, 2003), 131–47 (English trans.: *Truth and Tolerance: Christianity and World Religions* [San Francisco, 2004]).

[3] "The law of nature is that which nature teaches all sentient beings."—On the three dimensions of the medieval natural law (the dynamism of Being as a whole; the orientation of that nature which is common to men and animals [Ulpian]; and the specific orientation of the rational nature of man), see the information in the article by P. Delhaye, "Naturrecht", in *Lexikon für Theologie und Kirche*, 2nd ed., vol. 7, cols. 821–25. The concept of natural law found at the beginning of the *Decretum Gratiani* is noteworthy: "Humanum genus duobus regitur, naturali videlicet iure, et moribus. Ius naturale est, quod in lege et Evangelio continetur, quo quisque iubetur, alii facere, quod sibi vult fieri, et prohibetur, alii inferre, quod sibi nolit fieri" (The human race is governed by two things, namely, the natural law and customs. The natural law is that which is contained in the law and in the gospel, whereby each one is commanded to do to another what he wishes to be done to himself and is forbidden to inflict on another what he does not wish to be done to himself).

those specifically human tasks that the reason of man has created and that cannot be resolved without the reason.

One final element of the natural law that claimed (at least in the modern period) that it was ultimately a rational law has remained, namely, *human rights*. These are incomprehensible without the presupposition that man *qua* man, thanks simply to his membership in the species "man", is the subject of rights and that his being bears within itself values and norms that must be discovered—but not invented. Today, we ought perhaps to amplify the doctrine of human rights with a doctrine of human obligations and of human limitations. This could help us to grasp anew the relevance of the question of whether there might exist a rationality of nature and, hence, a rational law for man and for his existence in the world. And this dialogue would necessarily be intercultural today, both in its structure and in its interpretation. For Christians, this dialogue would speak of the creation and the Creator. In the Indian world, this would correspond to the concept of Dharma, the inner law that regulates all Being; in the Chinese tradition, it would correspond to the idea of the structures ordained by heaven.

4. The intercultural dimension and its consequences

Before I attempt to draw conclusions, I should like to widen the perspective I have indicated up to this point. If we are to discuss the basic questions of human existence today, the intercultural dimension seems to me absolutely essential—for such a discussion cannot be carried on exclusively either within the Christian realm or within the Western rational tradition. Both of these regard themselves as universal, and they may perhaps be universal *de iure*. De facto, however, they are obliged to acknowledge that they are accepted only by parts of mankind, and that they are comprehensible only in parts of mankind—although the number of competitors is of course much smaller than an initial glance might suggest.

The most important point in this context is that there no longer exists any uniformity within the individual cultural spheres, since they are all marked by profound tensions within their own cultural tradition. This is very obvious in the West. Although the secular culture is largely dominated by the strict rationality of which Jürgen Habermas has given us an impressive picture, a rationality that understands itself to be the element that binds people together, the Christian understanding of reality continues to be a powerful force. The closeness and the tension between these two poles varies: sometimes they are willing to learn from each other, but sometimes they reject each other to a greater or lesser degree.

The Islamic cultural sphere, too, is marked by similar tensions. There is a broad spectrum between the fanatical absolutism of a Bin Laden and attitudes that are open to a tolerant rationality. The third great cultural sphere, that of India—or, more precisely, the cultural spheres of

Hinduism and Buddhism—is likewise marked by similar tensions, although these take a less dramatic form (at
least to our eyes). These cultures, too, experience the
confrontation with the claims of Western rationality and
the questions posed by the Christian faith, since both
Western rationality and the Christian faith are present
there; they assimilate one or the other in various ways,
while still trying to preserve their own identity. We can
round off the picture by mentioning the tribal cultures
of Africa and the tribal cultures of Latin America that
have been summoned to new life by various Christian
theologies of liberation. In many ways, these seem to
call Western rationality into question; and this means
that they also call into question the universal claim of
Christian revelation.

What are the consequences of all this? The first point,
I believe, is that although the two great cultures of the
West, that is, the culture of the Christian faith and that
of secular rationality, are an important contributory factor (each in its own way) throughout the world and in
all cultures, nevertheless they are de facto not universal. This means that the question put by Jürgen Habermas' colleague in Teheran seems to me not devoid of
significance—namely, the question of whether a com-
parative study of cultures and the sociology of religion
suggest that European secularization is an exceptional
development and one that needs to be corrected. I
would not necessarily reduce this question to the mood
of Carl Schmitt, Martin Heidegger, and Levi Strauss,

that is, to a situation in which Europeans have grown weary of rationality.

At any rate, it is a fact that our secular rationality may seem very obvious to our reason, which has been formed in the West; but *qua* rationality, it comes up against its limitations when it attempts to demonstrate itself. The proof for it is in reality linked to specific cultural contexts, and it must acknowledge that it cannot as such be reproduced in the whole of mankind. This also means that it cannot be completely operative in the whole of mankind. In other words, the rational or ethical or religious formula that would embrace the whole world and unite all persons does not exist; or, at least, it is unattainable at the present moment. This is why the so-called "world ethos" remains an abstraction.

5. Conclusions

What, then, ought we to do? With regard to the practical consequences, I am in broad agreement with Jürgen Habermas' remarks about a postsecular society, about the willingness to learn from each other, and about self-limitation on both sides. At the end of my lecture, I should like to summarize my own view in two theses.

1. We have seen that there exist *pathologies in religion* that are extremely dangerous and that make it necessary to see the divine light of reason as a "controlling

organ". Religion must continually allow itself to be purified and structured by reason; and this was the view of the Church Fathers, too.[4] However, we have also seen in the course of our reflections that there are also *pathologies of reason*, although mankind in general is not as conscious of this fact today. There is a hubris of reason that is no less dangerous. Indeed, bearing in mind its potential effects, it poses an even greater threat—it suffices here to think of the atomic bomb or of man as a "product". This is why reason, too, must be warned to keep within its proper limits, and it must learn a willingness to listen to the great religious traditions of mankind. If it cuts itself completely adrift and rejects this willingness to learn, this relatedness, reason becomes destructive.

Kurt Hübner has recently formulated a similar demand. He writes that such a thesis does not entail a "return to faith"; rather, it means "that we free ourselves from the blindness typical of our age, that is, the idea that faith has nothing more to say to contemporary man because it contradicts his humanistic idea of reason, Enlightenment, and freedom".[5] Accordingly, I would speak of a necessary relatedness between reason and faith and between reason and religion, which are called to

---

[4] I have attempted to set this out in greater detail in my book *Glaube—Wahrheit—Toleranz* (see n. 2 above). See also M. Fiedrowicz, *Apologie im frühen Christentum*, 2nd ed. (Paderborn, 2001).

[5] K. Hübner, *Das Christentum im Wettstreit der Weltreligionen* (Tübingen: Mohr Siebeck, 2003), 148.

purify and help one another. They need each other, and they must acknowledge this mutual need.

2. This basic principle must take on concrete form in practice in the intercultural context of the present day. There can be no doubt that the two main partners in this mutual relatedness are the Christian faith and Western secular rationality; one can and must affirm this, without thereby succumbing to a false Eurocentrism. These two determine the situation of the world to an extent not matched by another cultural force; but this does not mean that one could dismiss the other cultures as a kind of *quantité négligeable*. For a Western hubris of that kind, there would be a high price to pay—and, indeed, we are already paying a part of it. It is important that both great components of the Western culture learn to *listen* and to accept a genuine relatedness to these other cultures, too. It is important to include the other cultures in the attempt at a polyphonic relatedness, in which they themselves are receptive to the essential complementarity of reason and faith, so that a universal process of purifications (in the plural!) can proceed. Ultimately, the essential values and norms that are in some way known or sensed by all men will take on a new brightness in such a process, and therefore that which holds the world together can once again become an effective force in mankind.

PART THREE

RESPONSIBILITY FOR THE PEACE

Four Talks
on the Occasion of the Sixtieth Anniversary
of the Landing of the Allied Forces in France

I

In Search of Peace

Europe at war and after the war

On June 6, 1944, when the Allied troops began to land in France, which was occupied by the German Wehrmacht, it was for the whole world—but also for many, many Germans—a sign of hope that soon there would be peace and freedom in Europe. What had happened? A criminal and his fellow Party members had managed to seize power in Germany. And once the Party was in power, law and injustice became intertwined, one often being inextricably confused with the other, because the government headed by a criminal had also assumed the jurisdictional prerogatives of the State and of its ordinances. Thus it could, in a certain sense, demand from its citizens obedience to the law and respect for the authority of the State (cf. Rom 13:1ff.) while at the same time using the law as a means to criminal ends.

A conference given by Cardinal Ratzinger at the Church of Saint-Étienne in Caen, June 5, 2004. [Translated from French.]

The same legal order that continued to some extent to
function as usual in everyday life had become simultaneously a force that was destroying the law. The perversion of the ordinances that ought to have served the
cause of justice but instead were consolidating the rule
of injustice and making it inscrutable was in actual fact
a dominion of lies that darkened consciences. Facilitat-
ing this dominion of lies was a system of intimidation,
in which no one could confide in anyone else, because
everyone, in a way, had to protect himself under a mask
of lies that, on the one hand, served the purpose of self-
defense but tended, on the other hand, to strengthen the
power of evil. Thus it was necessary for the whole world
to intervene in order to break the cycle of criminality
and to reestablish liberty and law. We give thanks at this
hour that this indeed happened, and it is not only the
countries that were occupied by the German troops and
delivered from Nazi terror that give thanks. We Germans, too, give thanks that liberty and law were restored
to us through that military operation. If ever in history
there was a just war, this was it: the Allied intervention
ultimately benefited also those against whose country
the war was waged. Such an observation, it seems to
me, is important, because it demonstrates on the basis
of a historical event that absolute pacifism is unsustain-
able. This, of course, in no way diminishes the duty to
ask very carefully whether and under what conditions
something like a "just war" is still possible today: that is
to say, a military intervention conducted in the interests

of peace and according to moral criteria against unjust regimes. Above all, though, what we have said should make it quite clear, we hope, that peace and law, peace and justice are inseparably connected with each other. When law is trampled on and injustice comes to power, peace is always threatened and is already to some extent broken. In this sense a commitment to peace is above all a commitment to a form of law that guarantees justice for the individual and for the entire community.

In Europe, after the end of the hostilities, in March 1945, a long period of peace was granted to our continent, such as it has rarely experienced in all of its history. This is due in large measure to the first generation of politicians after the war—Churchill, Adenauer, Schumann, De Gasperi—whom we must thank in this hour. We must be grateful that the decisive factor in rebuilding the Western world after the war was ultimately not the thought of revenge or of humiliating the conquered, but rather the duty of guaranteeing the rights of all, so that instead of competition there would be collaboration, a reciprocal exchange, mutual acquaintance and friendship within a diversity in which each nation preserves its identity while sharing the responsibility to respect the law, after the previous perversion of it. The driving force behind this politics of peace was the connection between political action and morality. The inner criterion of all politics is found in those moral values which we do not invent but only recognize and which are the same for all men. Let us say it plainly: these politicians drew their moral concept of the State, of peace and responsibility, from their Christian faith, a faith that had overcome the challenges of the Enlightenment and to a great extent had been purified in its confrontation with the distortion of the law and of morality caused by the Party. They wanted to set up, not a denominational State but, rather, a State informed by ethical reasoning; still, their faith had helped them to revive and reestablish the rule of reason that had been subjected and perverted by an ideological tyranny. They developed a politics of reason—of moral reasoning; their Christianity had not distanced them from reason but rather had illuminated their reason.

Of course we should add the fact that Europe was divided by a border that cut not only our continent but also the entire world in two. A large part of Central and Eastern Europe found itself under the rule of an ideology that exploited the Party and subjected the State to the Party, thus transforming it into a party. Here, too, the result was a rule of lies and the destruction of mutual trust. Since the collapse of those dictatorships, we have seen what enormous economic, ideological, and spiritual disasters these regimes caused. In the Balkans, armed conflicts broke out in which the whole historical weight of the past provoked new explosions of violence. Although we emphasize the criminal character of these regimes and are glad that they have been overthrown, we must nevertheless ask ourselves why the majority of the African and Asian peoples, the so-called nonaligned states, considered the system in the East more moral and more realistic for their own political development than the political and legal order in the West. This no doubt indicates shortcomings in our political structures on which we should reflect.

The development of the world situation after the war

Although Europe since 1945, with the exception of the conflicts in the Balkans, has experienced a period of peace, the world situation overall has been anything but peaceful. From Korea to Vietnam, from India to Pakistan, in Bangladesh, Algeria, and the Congo, from Nigeria (Biafra) to the hostilities in the Sudan, Rwanda and Burundi, Ethiopia, Somalia, Mozambique, Angola, Liberia, and in Afghanistan and Chechnya, a blood-stained arc of armed conflicts has developed, to which must be added the battles in and for the Holy Land and in Iraq. This is not the place to analyze and classify these conflicts, the wounds from which are still bleeding. I would like to examine in more detail, however, two phenomena that are in a certain sense new, because in them a specific threat comes to light and, along with it, the particular task of our times in the search for peace.

One of these phenomena is the sudden apparent decline in the cohesive force of the law and in the ability of different communities to coexist. A typical example, it seems to me, of the breakdown of the force of the law that plunges society into chaos and anarchy is Somalia.

But Liberia, too, presents an example of the way in which a society disintegrates from within because the national government is incapable of establishing its credibility as a force for peace and freedom, and therefore everyone tries to take justice into his own hands. We witnessed something similar in Europe after the collapse of the united Yugoslav government. Ethnic populations that for generations, despite many tensions, had lived together peaceably suddenly rose up against each other with an unimaginable cruelty. It was like a breach in a spiritual dam: the protective barrier no longer withstood the pressures of a new situation, and the arsenal of hostility and violence that lurked in the depths of men's souls, held back until then by the forces of law and of a common history, exploded without restraints. Of course, in that region different historical traditions, among which there had always been latent tensions, lived side by side: there both Latin and Greek forms of Christianity could be found in addition to the active presence of Islam, thanks to centuries of Turkish rule. But all these tensions had not prevented a peaceful coexistence that now was disintegrating and headed for anarchy. How could it happen? How was it possible that suddenly, in Rwanda, the coexistence between the Hutu and Tutsi tribes turned into bloody hostilities everywhere? There were certainly many causes for that collapse of law and of the capacity for reconciliation. We can mention several. Cynicism and ideology had darkened consciences in all these regions: the promises of ideology justified any and all means that might seem suited to its purposes, thus abolishing, so to speak, the very idea of law or even the distinction between good and evil. Besides the cynicism of the ideologies (and often closely connected with it) there is the cynicism of business interests and of the major markets, the shameless exploitation of the earth's natural resources. Here, too, the common good is set aside by the profit motive, and power takes the place of law. In this way the positive influence of ethics dissolves from within, and finally the material advantage that was being pursued is itself destroyed. At this level we are confronted with a major task for Christians today: we must begin by learning from each other to want to be reconciled and to do everything possible to ensure that conscience has an authoritative voice, instead of being crushed by ideology and financial interests. Especially in the Balkans (although the same thing is true for Ireland), the task of genuine ecumenism should be to seek together the peace of Christ, to offer it to one another, and thus to consider the very ability to make peace as a genuine criterion for truth.

The other phenomenon that weighs heavily on us especially today is terrorism, which meanwhile has become a sort of new world war—a war with no definite front, which can strike everywhere and no longer recognizes the distinction between combatants and the civilian population, between the guilty and the innocent. Given the fact that terrorist agents, or even conventional organized crime (which is constantly strengthening and extending its network), could gain access to nuclear arms and biological weapons, the peril that threatens us has reached frightening dimensions. As long as this potential for destruction remained exclusively in the hands of the major powers, one could always hope that reason and the awareness of the dangers weighing upon the people and the State would rule out the use of this type of weaponry. Indeed, despite all the tensions between East and West, we were spared a full-scale war, thanks be to God. But in dealing with the terrorist forces and organized crime, we can no longer count on such reasoning, because the readiness to engage in self-destruction is one of the basic components of terrorism—a kind of self-destruction that is exalted as martyrdom and transformed into a promise.

In search of peace: The question of the right relation between reason and religion

What can we do, what must we do in this situation? First of all, we need to consider several fundamental truths. One cannot put an end to terrorism—a force that is opposed to the law and cut off from morality—solely by means of force. It is certain that, in defending the law against a force that aims to destroy law, one can and in certain circumstances must make use of proportionate force in order to protect it. An absolute pacifism that denies the law any and all coercive measures would be capitulation to injustice, would sanction its seizure of power, and would abandon the world to the dictates of violence, as we already explained briefly at the beginning. But in order to prevent the force of the law itself from becoming injustice, it must be subjected to strict criteria that should be acknowledged as such by all. It must inquire into the causes of terrorism, which very often is rooted in injustices that are not countered by effective measures. Therefore it must strive by all means to remove the preexisting injustices. Above all, it is important to offer forgiveness again and again in order to break the vicious circle of violence. Where the principle of "an eye for an eye" is ruthlessly put into practice, there is no way out of the violence. Humanitarian gestures, which break with violence and see a fellow man in the opponent and appeal to his own humanity, are necessary, even when they seem at first to be a waste of time. In all these cases it is important that there not be just one political power that maintains law and order. Particular interests then become too easily mixed up in the intervention and obscure the clear vision of justice. A genuine *ius gentium* [international law] is urgently necessary, without hegemonic dominion and its accompanying interventions: only in this way can it be evident that it is a matter of protecting the rights common to all, even those who find themselves, so to speak, on the opposite side. This is precisely what succeeded in convincing those who had fought against each other in World War II and brought about a true peace. It was a question by no means of reinforcing one particular law, but rather of establishing freedom for all and the rule of genuine law, even though, of course, this was not able to prevent the development of new hegemonic structures.

But in the present clash between the major democracies and Islamist terrorism, even more profound questions come into play. There seems to be a collision of two major cultural systems, which manifest, nevertheless, quite different forms of power and of moral perspective: the "West" and Islam. What is the West, however? And what is Islam? Each one is a complex world including great differences within it, and these two worlds are also, in many respects, mutually interactive. To that extent it is wrong to generalize in opposing the West and Islam. Yet some commentators tend to describe the contrast in even starker terms: enlightened reason, they say, is confronting here a fanatical, fundamentalist form of religion. Therefore, in their view, we must defeat fundamentalism in all its forms and promote the victory of reason so as to leave the coast clear for enlightened forms of religion (which are considered enlightened provided they are subject in everything to the standards of that reason).

It is true that in this situation the relationship between reason and religion is of decisive importance and that the search for the right balance between them is at the heart of our efforts on behalf of peace. Modifying a famous remark by Hans Küng ("Keine Weltfriede ohne Religionsfriede!" [There will be no peace in the world without peace among religions]), I would say that there can be no peace in the world without genuine peace between reason and faith, because without peace between reason and religion, the sources of morality and law dry up. To explain what I mean to say by this, I will formulate the same idea in negative terms. There are pathologies of religion, as we can see, and there are pathologies of reason, as we can also see. Both sorts of pathologies pose a fatal threat to peace, and even to mankind as a whole, in our age of global power structures. Let us look at this more closely. God or the Divinity can become a way of making absolute claims for one's own authority and interests. Such a partisan image of God, which identifies God's absolute character with a particular community or its areas of interest and thereby raises things that are empirical and relative to the status of absolutes, dissolves law and morality. Good is then whatever serves my own power, and the difference between good and evil collapses in practice. Morality and law become partisan. This is further aggravated when the will to fight for one's own causes acquires all the weight of absolutist fanaticism, of religious fanaticism, and thereby becomes brutal and blind. God is transformed into an idol in which man adores his own will. We can see something of this sort in the terrorists and their ideology of martyrdom, an ideology that, to tell the truth, in certain cases can also be quite simply an expression of despair in dealing with the injustice in the world. Furthermore, closer to home, in the sects of the Western world, we find examples of irrationalism and a distortion of the religious dimension that show how dangerous a religion that loses its bearings can be.

But there is also a pathology of reason that is entirely cut off from God. We have seen it in the totalitarian ideologies that cut themselves off from God and wanted henceforth to construct a new man, a new world. Hitler, certainly, must be described as an irrationalist. The major prophets and practitioners of Marxism, however, likewise considered themselves to be rebuilding the world based on reason alone. Perhaps the most dramatic example of this pathology of reason was Pol Pot, in whom the cruelty inherent in such a reconstruction of the world is quite evident. Spiritual developments in the West, too, are tending more and more toward devastating pathologies of reason. Did not the atomic bomb, with which reason sought power in the ability to destroy instead of being a constructive force, already overstep the boundaries? Furthermore, when reason gets its hands on the origins of life through research into the genetic code, it increasingly tends to see man no longer as a gift of the Creator (or of "Nature") but as a product. Man is "produced", and what we "produce" we can also destroy. Human dignity vanishes. In what, then, are human rights supposed to be anchored? How can we maintain respect for human life, for the disadvantaged, the weak, the suffering, and the disabled? At the same time the notion of reason is becoming more and more attenuated. For example, ancient philosophers distinguished between *ratio* and *intellectus*, between reason in relation to empirical reality and man-made things and that reason which penetrates the deepest levels of being. Now, only reason in the more restricted sense remains. Only what is verifiable or, more precisely, what can be proved, is said to be reasonable; reason is reduced to what can be confirmed by means of experimentation. The entire field of morality and religion is thus relegated to the domain of the "subjective"—it falls outside the scope of commonsense reason. Religion and morality no longer pertain to reason; there are no more common, "objective" criteria for morality. This is not viewed as being particularly tragic, in the case of religion: everyone has to choose his own. But this means that it is regarded, in any case, as a sort of subjective ornament that may have useful motives. In the study of morality, general rules are sought. Of course, if reality is nothing but the result of mechanical processes, then it contains no moral criteria. The "good in itself", which Kant was still so concerned about, no longer exists. "Good" simply means "better than", as it was once remarked by a moral theologian who is now deceased. But if that is so, then there is no longer anything that is always and in itself evil. Good and evil depend then on a calculus of consequences. And this is precisely how the ideological dictatorships have acted: in certain cases, if it is in the interest of building the future world of reason, it can be a good thing to kill innocent people. In any case, their absolute dignity no longer exists. Sick reason and manipulated religion eventually lead to the same result. To sick reason any statement about permanent values, every defense of reason's capacity to know truth, seems to be fundamentalism. Nothing remains but dissolution or "deconstruction", the key concept in the writings of Jacques Derrida. He "deconstructed" hospitality, democracy, the State, and finally even the idea of terrorism, only to find himself terror-stricken by the events of September 11. Reason that can no longer recognize anything but itself and what is empirically certain is paralyzed and selfdestructive.

Faith in God, the idea of God, can be manipulated, and then it becomes destructive: this is the risk that religion runs. But reason that cuts itself off from God completely and tries to confine him to the purely subjective realm loses its bearings and thus opens the door to the forces of destruction. Whereas the Enlightenment was searching for moral foundations that would be valid "etsi Deus non daretur" [even if God did not exist], we must invite our agnostic friends today to be open to a morality "si Deus daretur" [as if God did exist]. Kolakowski, drawing on his experiences in an atheistic, agnostic society, has demonstrated masterfully that without this absolute point of reference, man's action becomes lost in uncertainty and is inevitably at the mercy of the forces of evil.[1] As Christians, we are called today, certainly not to

[1] Leszek Kolakowski, *Religion: If There Is No God—On God, the Devil, Sin, and Other Worries of the So-Called Philosophy of Religion* (South Bend, Ind.: St. Augustine Press, 2001).

set limits to reason and to oppose it, but rather to refuse to reduce it to the level of practical reason and to defend instead its ability to perceive good and the One who is Good, what is holy and the One who is Holy. Only in this way can we fight a real battle on behalf of man and against inhumanity. Only reason that is still open to God, only reason that does not banish morality to the subjective sphere and does not reduce it to a calculus can counter the manipulation of the idea of God and the pathologies of religion and offer remedies.

The task of Christians

And so it is plain that Christians today face a great challenge. Their task and ours is to see to it that reason is fully functional, not just in the realm of technology and material progress in the world, but also and especially as a faculty of truth, promoting its capacity to recognize what is good, which is a necessary condition for law and therefore also a prerequisite for peace in the world. Our task as contemporary Christians is to make sure that our idea of God is not excluded from the debate about man. This idea of God has two essential characteristics: God himself is the Logos—the rational origin of all reality, the creative reason from which the world came forth and which is reflected in the world. God is Logos—meaning, reason, the Word—and therefore man complies with this Logos by keeping an open mind and defending a type of reason that is not blind to the moral dimensions of being. For *logos* means a reason that is not simply mathematical but is at the same time the foundation and guarantee of the good. Faith in God as Logos is also faith in the creative power of reason; it is faith in God the Creator, which means believing that man is created in the image of God and that he therefore shares in the inviolable dignity of God himself. Here the idea of human rights has its ultimate foundation, even though it has developed in various ways and has not always been well received over the course of history.

God is Logos. But there is a second characteristic. The Christian faith in God tells us also that God— eternal Reason—is Love. It tells us that he is not a being turned in on himself, without relations to others. Precisely because he is sovereign, because he is the Creator, because he embraces everything, he is Relation and he is Love. Faith in the Incarnation of God in Jesus Christ, and in his suffering and death for mankind, is the supreme expression of a conviction that the heart of all morality, the heart of being itself and its deepest principle, is love. This affirmation is the most resolute refusal of every ideology of violence; it is the true *apologia* for man and for God. Let us not forget, however, that the God of reason and of love is also the Judge of the world and of mankind—the guarantor of justice, to whom men must render an accounting. Given the temptations to power, it is a fundamental obligation to keep in mind the truth about the Judgment: every one of us must someday give an account. There is a justice that is not abolished by love. In the *Gorgias* of Plato we find a striking parable for it that is not nullified but rather fully validated by the Christian faith. Plato explains how the soul, after death, at last finds itself naked before the Judge. Now it no longer matters what rank it held in the world. Whether it is the soul of the king of Persia or of any other ruler, the Judge sees the scars of his perjuries and crimes:

> with which each action has stained him, and he is all crooked with falsehood and imposture, and has no straightness, because he has lived without truth. [The Judge sees that he is] full of all deformity and disproportion, which is caused by license and luxury and insolence and incontinence.... Or, again, he looks with admiration on the soul of some just one who has lived in holiness and truth; he may have been a [free] man or not, ... and sends it to the Isles of the Blessed.[2]

Wherever such convictions are strong, law and justice are also in force.

I would like to mention yet a third element of the Christian tradition that is of fundamental importance in the difficult circumstances of our time. The Christian faith—following the way shown to us by Jesus—banished the ideal of political theocracy. To put it in modern language, it promoted the secular character of the State, in

---

[2] Plato, *Gorgias* 525a–526c, trans. Benjamin Jowell; cf. Christoph Schönborn, *Gott sandte seinen Sohn: Christologie* (Paderborn, 2002), 339.

which Christians live together in freedom with those who hold other beliefs, united by the common moral responsibility founded on human nature, on the nature of justice. The Christian faith distinguishes this from the Kingdom of God, which does not and cannot exist in this world as a political reality, but rather comes into being through faith, hope, and charity and must transform the world from within. In the conditions of this world, the Kingdom of God is not a worldly kingdom but rather an appeal to man's freedom and a support for reason so that it can accomplish its task. This distinction is what is ultimately at stake in the temptations of Jesus: the rejection of political theocracy, the relative importance of the State, the law that is proper to reason and at the same time freedom of choice, with which every human being is endowed. In this sense the secular State is a result of the fundamental Christian decision, even though it took a long struggle to understand all of its consequences. This secular, "lay" character of the State includes by its very nature this balance between reason and religion that I tried to demonstrate earlier. Therefore it is also opposed to ideological secularism, which tries to establish a State run by reason alone, a State that is cut off from all historical roots and hence no longer recognizes any moral foundations other than those that are evident to that reason. Eventually it has nothing left but the positivistic criterion of the majority principle, leading to the decadence of a law governed by statistics. If the nations of the Western world were to commit themselves entirely to this path, they would be unable in the long run to resist the pressure of ideologies and political theocracies. A State, even a secular State, has the right and even the obligation to rely on the moral traditions in which it is rooted and which shaped it; it can and must acknowledge the fundamental values that made it what it is and without which it cannot survive. There is no such thing as an ahistorical State based on abstract reason.

In practice this means that we Christians must strive, together with all of our fellow citizens, to give law and justice a moral foundation inspired by fundamental Christian ideas, however the individual may interpret their origins and harmonize them with his entire life. But in order to make such common rational convictions possible, in order to prevent "right reason" from losing its sight, it is important for us to live out our own heritage with vigor and purity, so that it might be made visible and effective, with all its intrinsic power of persuasion, in society as a whole. I would like to conclude with the words of Kurt Hübner, a German philosopher from Kiel, which clearly express this concern:

> We will be able to avoid conflict with the cultures that are hostile to us today only on condition that, by becoming once again fully conscious of how deeply rooted our culture is in Christianity, we disprove their vehement reproach that we have forgotten God. Of course that will not be enough to dispel the resentment

caused by the superiority of the West in many fields
that shape broad sectors of life today, but it can play an
important role in extinguishing the flames of the religious conflagration that feeds on it.[3]

Indeed, if we do not recall the God of the Bible, the
God who has come close to us in Jesus Christ, we will
not find the path of peace.

[3] K. Hübner, *Das Christentum im Wettstreit der Weltreligionen* (Tübingen:
Mohr Siebeck, 2003), 148.

2

Faith in the Triune God, and Peace in the World

The feast of the Holy Trinity is different from all the other feasts of the liturgical year, such as Christmas, Epiphany, Easter, and Pentecost, when we celebrate the wondrous works of God in history: the Incarnation, the Resurrection, the Descent of the Holy Spirit, and consequently the birth of the Church. Today we are not celebrating an event in which "something" of God is made visible; rather, we are celebrating the very mystery of God. We rejoice in God, in the fact that he is the way he is; we thank him for existing; we are grateful that he is what he is and that we can know him and love him and that he knows and loves us and reveals himself to us. But the existence of God, his being, the fact that he knows us—is that really a cause for joy? Certainly it is not something easy to understand or experience. Many

A homily given in the Cathedral of Bayeux on the Feast of the Holy Trinity, June 6, 2004.

gods in the different religions of peoples throughout the world are terrible, cruel, selfish, an inscrutable mixture of good and evil. The ancient world was characterized by a fear of the gods and a dread of their mysterious power: it was necessary to win the favor of the gods, to act in such a way as to avoid their whims or their bad humor. Part of the Christian mission was a liberating force that was able to drive out a whole world of idols and gods that are now considered empty, illusory appearances. At the same time it proclaimed the God who, in Jesus, became man, the God who is Love and Reason. This God is mightier than all the dark powers that the world can contain: "We know that 'an idol has no real existence,' and that 'there is no God but one.' For although there may be so-called gods in heaven or on earth—as indeed there are many 'gods' and many 'lords'—yet for us there is one God, the Father, from whom are all things and for whom we exist" (1 Cor 8:4–6). Even today this is a revolutionary, liberating message with respect to all the ancient traditional religions: no longer is there reason to fear the spirits that surround us on all sides, coming and going ceaselessly, eluding our vain efforts at exorcism. Anyone who "dwells in the shelter of the Most High, who abides in the shadow of the Almighty" (Ps 91:1) knows that he is safe, guarded tenderly by the One who welcomes him and offers him refuge. Someone who knows the God of Jesus Christ knows that the other forms of fear in the presence of God have disappeared also, that he has overcome all the forms of harrowing existential anguish that spread through the world in ever new ways. In view of all the horrors of the world, the same question unceasingly arises: Does God exist? And if he exists, is he truly good? Might he not be instead a mysterious and dangerous reality? In modern times this question is posed differently: the existence of God seems to be a limit to our freedom. He is perceived as a sort of supervisor who pursues us with his glance. In the modern era, the rebellion against God assumes the form of a fear of an omnipresent, all-seeing God. His glance appears as a threat to us; indeed, we prefer not to be seen; we just want to be ourselves and nothing more. Man does not feel free, he does not feel that he is truly himself, until God is set aside. The story of Adam already notes this: he sees God as a competitor. Adam wants to lead his own life, all alone, and tries to hide from God "among the trees of the garden" (Gen 3:8). Sartre, too, declared that we must deny God, even if he must exist philosophically, because the concept of God is opposed to man's freedom and greatness.

But has the world really become brighter, freer, happier after setting God aside? Or has man not been stripped of his own dignity and condemned to an empty freedom that makes cruel and ruthless choices of all sorts? God's glance frightens us only if we think of him as reducing us to some kind of servitude or slavery; but if we read in it the expression of his love, we discover that he is the fundamental requirement for our very being, that it is he who makes us live. "He who has seen me has seen the Father", Jesus said to Philip and to us all (Jn 14:9). Jesus' face is the face of God himself: this is what God is like. Jesus suffered for us, and by his death he has given us peace; he reveals to us who God is. His glance, far from being a threat, is a glance that saves us.

Yes, we can rejoice that God exists, that he has revealed himself to mankind, and that he does not leave us alone. How consoling it is to know the telephone number of a friend, to know good people who love us, who are always available and never aloof: at any time we can call them and they can call us. This is precisely what the Incarnation of God in Christ says to us: God has written our names and phone numbers in his address book! He is always listening; we do not need money or technology to call him. Thanks to baptism and confirmation, we are privileged to belong to his family. He is always ready to welcome us: "Behold, I am with you always, to the close of the age" (Mt 28:20).

But the Gospel reading for today adds a particularly important statement: Jesus promises the Holy Spirit (Jn 16:13), whom he calls, several times, the "Paraclete". What does that mean? In Latin, the word is translated as *Consolator*, the Comforter. Etymologically, the Latin word means: the one who stays by us when we feel lonely. Thus our solitude ceases to be loneliness. For a human being, solitude is often a place of unhappiness; he needs love, and solitude makes the absence of it conspicuous. Loneliness indicates a lack of love; it is something that threatens our quality of life at the deepest level. Not being loved is at the core of human suffering and personal sadness. The word *Consoler* tells us precisely that we are not alone, that we can never feel abandoned by Love. By the gift of the Holy Spirit, God has entered into our loneliness and has shattered it. Indeed, this is genuine consolation; it does not consist merely of words but has the force of an active and effective reality. During the Middle Ages this definition of the Spirit as Consoler led to the Christian duty of entering into the solitude of those who suffer. The first hospices and hospitals were dedicated to the Holy Spirit: thus men undertook the mission of continuing the Spirit's work; they dedicated themselves to being "consolers", to entering into the solitude of the sick, the suffering, and the elderly, so as to bring them light.

This is still a serious duty for us today, in our time.

Moreover, the Greek work *parakletos* can be translated in yet another way: it also means "advocate". A verse from the Book of Revelation might help us to understand it better: "And I heard a loud voice in heaven, saying, 'Now the salvation and the power and the kingdom of our God and the authority of his Christ have come, for the accuser of our brethren has been thrown down, who accuses them day and night before our God'" (Rev 12:10). Someone who does not love God with all his heart does not love man, either. Those who deny God quickly become persons who destroy nature and accuse men, because accusing other men and nature enables them to justify their opposition to God: a God who has made this cannot be good! That is their logic. The Holy Spirit, the Spirit of God, is not an accuser; he is an advocate and defender of mankind and creation. God himself takes the side of men and creatures. Within creation, God affirms and defends himself by coming to our defense. God is for us; we see that clearly throughout the earthly life of Jesus: he is the only one who takes our side, becomes one with us even unto death. Saint Paul's awareness of this prompted an outburst of joy:

> If God is for us, who is against us? ... Who shall bring any charge against God's elect? It is God who justifies; who is to condemn? Is it Christ Jesus, who died, yes, who was raised from the dead, who is at the right hand of God, who indeed intercedes for us? ... For I am sure that neither death, nor life, nor angels, nor principalities, nor things present, nor things to come, nor powers, nor height, nor depth, nor anything else in all creation, will be able to separate us from the love of God in Christ Jesus our Lord. (Rom 8:31–39)

This God is for us a cause of joy, and we want to celebrate him. To know him and to acknowledge him is of great importance in our time. We are remembering the terrible days of the Second World War, happy that the dictator Hitler has disappeared along with all his atrocities and that Europe has been able to regain its freedom. But we cannot forget the fact that, even today, the world suffers from atrocious threats and cruelties. To corrupt and exploit the image of God is as dangerous as the denial of God that was part and parcel of the twentieth-century ideologies and of the totalitarian regimes that sprang from them, turning the world into an arid desert, outside and inside, to the very depths of the soul. Precisely at this historical moment, Europe and the world need the presence of God that was revealed in Jesus; they need God to stay close to mankind through the Holy Spirit. It is part of our responsibility as Christians to see to it that God remains in our world, that he is present to it as the one and only force capable of preserving mankind from self-destruction.

God is One and Three: he is not an eternal solitude; rather, he is an eternal love that is based on the reciprocity of the Persons, a love that is the first cause, the origin, and the foundation of all being and of every form of life. Unity engendered by love, trinitarian unity, is a unity infinitely more profound than the unity of a building stone, indivisible as that may be from a material perspective.

This supreme unity is not rigidly static; it is love. The most beautiful artistic depiction of this mystery was left to us by Andrei Rublev in the fifteenth century: the world-renowned icon of the Trinity. Of course, it does not portray the eternal mystery of God in himself; who would dare to do that? It attempts, rather, to represent this mystery as it is reflected in the gift of itself in history, as in the visit of the three men to Abraham by the oaks of Mamre (Gen 18:1–33). Abraham immediately recognized that they were not just like any other men, but that God himself was coming to him through them. In Rublev's icon, the mystery of this event is made visible, presented as an event that can be contemplated in its many dimensions: thus the mystery as such is respected. The artistic richness of this icon allows me to underscore another characteristic: the natural surroundings of this event, which express the mystery of the Persons. We are near the oaks of Mamre, which Rublev depicts in stylized form as a single tree representing the tree of life; and this tree of life is none other than the trinitarian love that created the world, sustains it, saves it, and is the source of all life. We see also the tent, the dwelling of Abraham, which recalls the Prologue of John's Gospel: "And the Word became flesh and dwelt among us" (Jn 1:14). The body of the incarnate Word of God became itself the tent, the place where God dwells: God becomes our refuge and our dwelling place. Finally, the gift that Abraham offers, "a calf, tender and good", is replaced, in the icon, with a cup, a symbol of the Eucharist, a sign of the gift in which God gives himself: "Love, sacrifice, and self-immolation preceded the act by which the world was created and are the source of that creation."[1] The tree, the tent, and the cup: these elements show us the mystery of God, allow us to immerse ourselves in the contemplation of its intimate depths, in his trinitarian love. This is the God that we celebrate. This is the God who gives us joy. He is the true hope of our world. Amen.

---

[1] P. Evdokimov, *The Art of the Icon: A Theology of Beauty*, trans. Steven Bigham (Redondo Beach, Calif.: Oakwood Publications, 1990), 247.

3

The Responsibility of Christians
for Peace

On this day, June 6, we remember the battle for Europe
and for its freedom that entered into its crucial phase
sixty years ago. But our commemoration does not look
only to the past; it should also be an orientation toward
the future.

But first let us pause for a moment and look back.
Sixty years ago armies fought to liberate Europe and the
world from a brutal dictatorship that despised human
beings. The human person was trampled on, exploited,
treated as an object by the madness of a regime that
wanted to create a new world. People spoke about God,
but his name was used as a slogan that served the will of
an absolute power. God's will did not count; what mat-
tered instead was one's personal will to power, which
no longer recognized in man the image of God that
deserved respect but simply considered him as "human

A speech given at the ecumenical service in the Cathedral of Bayeux on
June 6, 2004.

material" to be exploited; in fact, man was disdained and disfigured in exactly the same way as God himself was being disdained and disfigured. Countless persons were used as raw material in the concentration camps. A vast array of young men fell on the battlefields; today we are here to honor their graves. We know that all those who fell on both sides are now in the merciful goodness of God. They are all children of God; each one is personally known by God, is loved and willed by him, is called by name. Every single person left an empty space behind; for each of them there were so many tears and so much sorrow. But we know that now they are in good hands; they are in God's hands, in his goodness, which is mercy and reconciliation. Today this should be for us a heritage that helps us to consider anew the dignity of man, of every human person; it helps us to reflect in a new way on death and on eternal life. We must learn to recognize the image of God in the face of every man, however disagreeable or strange he may seem to us. In every human being we should see a companion in the life hereafter, a fellow traveler whom we will meet again in the next world. And we should foster a new awareness of our vocation to eternal life, living in such a way that we will be able to meet God face to face and present to him our earthly life. For the generation to which I belong, the idea of the hereafter and of eternal life was increasingly set aside and considered marginal, even in the preaching of the Church. Perhaps both the faithful and those who proclaimed the Word were afraid that thinking too much about the hereafter would cause Christians to neglect this world and its concrete, historic realities. It seemed that Christians were only half-heartedly concerned with building up this world. For centuries it had been said that life would be better and more humane if Christians did not live as though they had to flee the world. And then people imagined there would be plenty of time, in any case, to think about the hereafter, whereas the present moment was worth the trouble of striving to make the world more livable at last. But surely the world has not become more livable or more humane as a result of this ideology; on the contrary, the person who lives the present moment in light of his responsibility with regard to eternal life is the one who gives full meaning to these present days. The parable of the talents shows us that the Lord has not called us to a life of comfortable tranquility; rather, he has called us to trade with the talents that have been given to us and to increase them (see Mt 25:14–30). Furthermore, to live with the thought of eternal life is to be free of the desire to enjoy everything right away, to use up everything right away; for then one knows that now is the time to work and afterward comes the great feast. These cemeteries before which we stand today exhort us to remember death and thus invite us to live the present moment well with a view to eternity.

There are three key words that could very well sum up our reflection: reconciliation, peace, and responsibility. After the bloody confrontations of the Second

World War, a process of reconciliation began, for which we are deeply grateful, with heartfelt appreciation. The United States undertook a vast and compelling program of foreign aid to help their former adversaries get back on their feet and to promote reconstruction. Great Britain and France shook hands as a sign of reconciliation with those who had been their enemies during World War II. Charles de Gaulle once explained the meaning of this: although there was a time when it was our duty to be enemies, now it is our joy that we can be friends. The process of reconciliation that has taken place in Europe, thanks in particular to the North Atlantic Treaty Organization, has changed the course of world history; this process has its origins in the Christian spirit.

Only reconciliation can create peace; it is not violence that can resolve situations, but rather justice. This must be the normative criterion for all political action in the conflicts of the present time. The Letter to the Hebrews speaks about Christ's blood, which utters a cry different from the one that came from the blood of Abel (12:24). This cry calls, not for retaliation and revenge, but for reconciliation. The Letter to the Ephesians speaks to us about this same reality: Christ is our peace. By his death he has broken down the wall of separation and enmity. By his blood, which is to say, by his love, which extends unto death and endures even in the experience of death, he unites those who were far off and those who were near (cf. Eph 2:14–22). This is the God whom we proclaim, and this is the image of man that should guide us.

The peace of Christ surpasses the boundaries of Christianity and is valid for all, both near and far. Our ways of acting, both in little things and in great matters, should proceed from him as their source and bear his imprint. And with that, we come to the final key word of our reflection: the word "responsibility". Already with the conclusion of World War I and even more forcefully after the experience of World War II, the cry arose: "War never again!" Unfortunately, the reality has proved to be quite different: the decades following 1945 were afflicted with bloody wars in various parts of the world. And unfortunately we must fear that evil injustice will rear its head once more and that it might again be necessary to defend law and justice against evil and injustice, even by resorting to military measures. What, then, can we hope for? What should we do? The totalitarian ideologies of the twentieth century promised us that they would build a free and just world, and in order to reach that objective they demanded the slaughter of countless victims. But the utopian dream has exerted a powerful attraction on the Christian consciousness and left a deep impression on it. The expectation of Christ's return refers to a salvation that takes place beyond history, whereas people want a hope within history and for the sake of history. They prefer to remove the word "God" from the New Testament expression "the Kingdom of God" and to speak only about the "kingdom" to describe a new utopia that embraces both Christians and non-Christians: the "kingdom", that is, a better world has to come about within history. Nothing else about our faith is preached, then, and the prescriptions for building this "kingdom" are rather indefinite, so that they are open to any ideological misinterpretation. But utopias and ideologies are deceptive phantasms that lead men into error. And once again we ask ourselves: "What is being promised us?" "What should we do?"

The Christian answer involves three aspects. First there is the promise of the heavenly Jerusalem that is not built by men but is given by God. Connected with it, in a manner that transcends history, is the ancient prophecy that human freedom would time and again be misused, and so evil would time and again gain power in the world. The Book of Revelation expresses this by means of terrifying images. Beyond the obscurity of these images we can catch a glimpse of the other side of the story, which is essential: even though God allows a lot of room to the freedom that chooses evil (there are all too many proofs of this, different ones in every age), he will never let the world fall completely out of his hands. Although the Book of Revelation speaks about destruction, it is for a limited time, and in a certain sense disaster strikes only a relatively small percentage, for instance, one-third.

The world belongs to God and not to the Evil One, however much territory the latter may acquire. This certitude is fundamental, and it is a decisive point in the apocalyptic imagery. Indeed, it presupposes that the earth-shaking events narrated in the Book of Revelation are already well known; they will never manage to take complete possession of the world and will never succeed in destroying it: this is the real heart of the message.

Finally, the third aspect of the Christian response to the question regarding the future is called *ethics* or responsibility. This is not the magic charm of a progressive historical development that tends to build a world that is finally just, even though it may have to be without freedom. God sustains the world, but he does this essentially by means of our freedom; this should be freedom to do good, which is capable of opposing freedom to do evil. Faith does not create a better world, but it awakens and strengthens those ethical forces that construct embankments and bulwarks against the tide of evil. Faith awakens the freedom to do good and fortifies it against the temptation to use freedom in a distorted way to choose evil. The graves of the Second World War commend to us the task of strengthening the forces of good: it is an invitation to work, to live, and to suffer for the propagation and reinforcement of those values and truths that build a united world with God as its fulcrum. God promised Abraham that he would not destroy the city of Sodom if at least ten just men could be found there (Gen 18:32). We must make sure, then, that there will never be a day without those ten just men who can save an entire city.

4

The Grace of Reconciliation

This is the moment to get down on our knees with the utmost respect for those who died in World War II, remembering the countless young men from our country who, along with their future and their hopes, were destroyed in the bloody massacre of the war. And as Germans we are grieved by the fact that their idealism, their enthusiasm, and their loyalty to the State were exploited by an unjust regime.

But this does not stain the honor of those young men; only God was able to look into their conscience. Every one of them stands before God as an individual, with the course of his life and with his death; each one stands before the God whose merciful goodness, as we know, protects all our dead. They sought only to do their duty, and often this involved tremendous interior struggles, with many doubts and questions. But they look at us and question us: "And you? What will you do so that

A speech given in the German cemetery of La Cambe in Caen on June 5, 2004.

young men will no longer be forced to go to war? What will you do so that the world will not be devastated again by hatred, violence, and lies?"

But although this is an hour for sorrow and an examination of conscience, it is also a moment for profound gratitude, because over these graves reconciliation was born. Former enemies became friends, and now they walk hand in hand along their common path. The sacrifice of our dead was not in vain, even if we consider it solely from the perspective of history. After the First World War rancor and hostility remained among the nations that had fought one another, especially between the French and the Germans. This hatred poisoned souls. The Treaty of Versailles had deliberately planned to humiliate Germany and impose enormous burdens on it, which reduced its people to dire straits, thus opening the door to extremist ideologies and dictatorship. Those lying promises to restore Germany to its freedom, dignity, honor, and greatness spread widely and gained a hearing. But, as we have seen, the principle of "an eye for an eye, a tooth for a tooth" cannot lead to peace. Thank God, nothing like that happened again after World War II. With the Marshall Plan, the Americans provided enormous amounts of foreign aid to us Germans, enabling us to rebuild our country and fostering its freedom and well-being. In the new world order that followed the collapse of colonialism, and during the extremely difficult period of the "Cold War" between East and West, people quickly realized that only a united

Europe could have a say in history and in its own future. They understood that the various nationalist ideologies that had torn apart our continent must vanish so as to make room for a new solidarity. And so it happened after the conflicts between France and Germany, which for centuries had left their bloody mark. Thanks be to God, an increasingly close friendship has been established between the French and the Germans, and thus, since the late 1950s, Europe has developed, starting with that central unity and then expanding in ever larger circles. And today we stand before these graves that remind us of the fatal discord of the past, but now we are here as friends, as persons who have been reconciled with one another.

As we look back now on the process of mutual reconciliation and gradually developing solidarity, it appears to us as a logical development that was demanded and made structurally possible by the new world order. But we cannot overlook the fact that this logic per se was not understood in the same way by all and was not self-actualizing. History shows us that too often men act in ways contrary to all logic and reason. The fact that the politics of reconciliation triumphed is to the credit of a whole generation of politicians: let us recall the names of Adenauer, Schumann, De Gasperi, De Gaulle. These were objective, intelligent men who had a healthy political realism. But their realism was rooted in the firm ground of the Christian *ethos*, which they recognized as an *ethos* of reason, an *ethos* of enlightened, refined reason.

They knew very well that politics cannot be mere prag-matism but must be a moral endeavor: the objective of politics is justice and, along with justice, peace. The political order and power itself must acknowledge their origins in the fundamental criteria of the law. But if the essence of politics is making power moral, along with the order that has the principles of law as its source, then in this twofold foundation we find a fundamental ethi-cal category. But where do the fundamental criteria of justice come from? Where can we find them? For these men it was quite clear that the Ten Commandments are the fundamental point of reference for justice, a refer-ence that is valid for all times; and they had reread, elab-orated, and reinterpreted this reference in the light of the Christian message. There is no disputing the histori-cal role of the Christian faith in giving life to Europe. It is to the great credit of Christianity that it gave birth to Europe after the decline of the Greco-Roman Empire and after the period of the barbarian invasions. Not only that, but the rebirth of Europe after World War II was likewise rooted in Christianity and, therefore, in man's responsibility before God: we are very much aware that this is the deepest foundation of a government of laws, as it is clearly stipulated in the German Constitution that was framed after the collapse of Nazism. Anyone who wants to build Europe today as a bastion of law and jus-tice that is valid for all men of all cultures cannot rely on an abstract reason that knows nothing about God and belongs to no particular culture, an abstract reason that

pretends to measure all cultures according to the yardstick of its own judgment. But what yardstick are they
talking about? What sort of freedom can reason of this
sort safeguard? What can it reject? Even today, responsibility before God and being rooted in the great values
and truths of the Christian faith—values that transcend
the individual Christian denominations because they are
common to all—are indispensable forces in the construction of a unified Europe that is much more than a
single economic bloc: a community of law, a bastion of
law, not only for itself but also for all of mankind.

The dead of La Cambe call to us: they rest in the
peace of God, but they continue to ask us: "What are
you doing for peace?" They warn us that the State is
capable of losing its foundations in law and of cutting
itself off from its roots. The memory of the sorrow and
of the evils of the Second World War, together with the
memory of the great work of reconciliation that, thank
God, has been accomplished in Europe, shows us where
to find those forces that can heal Europe and the world.
The earth can be a brighter place and the world can be
humane only if we let God into the world.

EPILOGUE

The Church and the Scandal
of Sexual Abuse

By Pope Emeritus Benedict XVI

On February 21 to 24, at the invitation of Pope Francis, the presidents of the world's bishops' conferences gathered at the Vatican to discuss the current crisis of the Faith and of the Church—a crisis felt throughout the world after distressing revelations of clerical abuse against minors. The extent and gravity of the reported incidents have deeply distressed priests and lay people alike, leading more than a few to call into question the very Faith of the Church. Here, a strong sign and a new beginning were necessary in order to render the Church truly credible once again as a light among peoples and as a helping force against the powers of destruction.

Since I myself had served in a position of responsibility as shepherd of the Church at the moment of the public outbreak of the crisis, as well as during its escalation, I had to ask myself what I, looking at the past, could contribute to [such] a new

This translation is based on the one by Anian Christoph Wimmer, which was originally published by the Catholic News Agency on April 10, 2019.

beginning—even though, as pope emeritus, I no longer directly carry the responsibility. Thus, after the meeting of the presidents of the bishops' conferences was announced, I compiled some notes in order to make a suggestion or two to help in this difficult hour. After some contact with Secretary of State Cardinal [Pietro] Parolin and the Holy Father [Pope Francis] himself, it seems appropriate to me to publish this text in the Klerusblatt *["Clergy Journal", a monthly periodical for clergy in Bavaria].*

My work is divided into three parts.

*In the first, I aim to present rather briefly the question's wider social context, without which the problem cannot be understood. I try to show that in the 1960s a colossal event took place that, in its scale, was practically unprecedented in history. One could say that in the twenty years from 1960 to 1980, the normative standards on sexuality that had held up to that point, collapsed entirely, and a new norm-lessness [*Normlosigkeit*] arose that many people have since worked hard to disrupt.*

In the second part, I try to indicate the effects of this situation on the formation of priests and on the lives of priests.

Finally, in the third part, I would like to put forth some perspectives for a proper response on the part of the Church.

I.

1.

The matter begins with the state-mandated and state-financed introduction of children and young people to the nature of sexuality. In Germany, the then–minister of health, Ms. (Käte) Strobel, commissioned an educational film showcasing everything that before now could not be shown in public, including sexual intercourse. Then what at first had been intended only for the sexual education of young people subsequently became accepted as a regular possibility, as though it were a given.

The *Sexkoffer* issued by the Austrian government [a controversial "suitcase" of sex education materials used in Austrian schools in the late 1980s] had similar effects. Sexual and pornographic films then became such an everyday reality that they were screened at dollar theaters [*Bahnhofskinos*]. I still remember walking through the city of Regensburg one day and seeing crowds of people standing and waiting in front of a big movie theater—a phenomenon that before then we had seen only during wartime [at groceries and dry goods stores] when some special ration was to be hoped for. Also lodged in my memory is arriving in the city on Good Friday and seeing all the billboards plastered with a large poster of two completely naked people in a tight embrace.

Among those freedoms that the Revolution of 1968 sought to fight for, there also stood this all-out sexual freedom, one which no longer admitted any norms. The propensity for violence that characterized these years was closely linked to this psychic collapse. In fact, sex films were no longer allowed on airplanes, since violent behavior would break out among the little community of passengers. Because the excesses of dress in that period likewise provoked aggression, school administrators also tried to introduce school uniforms, with a view to fostering a climate of learning. Part of the physiognomy of the Revolution of '68 was that even pedophilia was diagnosed as permissible and appropriate. For the young people in the Church, though not for them only, this was in many ways a very difficult time. I have always wondered how young people within this situation could approach and accept the priesthood, with all its consequences. These developments resulted in a sharp decline in priestly vocations and an upsurge in laicizations over the next few decades.

2.

At the same time, independently of this phenomenon, Catholic moral theology suffered a collapse that rendered the Church defenseless against these happenings in society. I will try to outline briefly the trajectory of this development. Until the Second Vatican Council, Catholic moral theology was broadly founded on natural law, with Sacred Scripture cited only for background or substantiation. In the Council's struggle for a new understanding of revelation, the natural law option was laid largely aside, and a moral theology based entirely on the Bible was demanded.

I still remember how the Jesuit faculty in Frankfurt had one highly gifted young Father ([Bruno] Schüller) lay the groundwork for developing a morality based

entirely on Scripture. Father Schüller's beautiful disser-
tation shows a first step toward building up a morality
grounded in Scripture. Father Schüller was then sent
to America for further studies and came back with the
realization that morality could not be systematically presented on the basis of the Bible alone. He then attempted
a more pragmatic moral theology, without thereby being
able to provide a response to the crisis of morality.

In the end, what broadly prevailed was the hypothesis that morality was to be determined exclusively by
the purposes of human action. While this crude strain
[of morality] did not endorse the old phrase "the end
justifies the means", this form of thought had become a
decisive influence. Consequently, there could no longer
be anything thoroughly good, much less anything cate-
gorically evil, but only relative value judgments. There
was no longer the Good, but only the relatively Better,
contingent on the moment and the circumstances.

The crisis of justifying and presenting Catholic
morality reached dramatic proportions in the late '80s
and the '90s. On January 5, 1989, the "Cologne Decla-
ration" appeared, signed by fifteen Catholic professors
of theology. It focused on various crisis points in the
relationship between the episcopal teaching office and
the task of theology. [Reactions to] this text, which at
first did not extend beyond the usual measure of pro-
tests, grew very rapidly into an outcry against the Magisterium of the Church and—with much uproar, both
audible and visible—gathered up from across the globe

the potential for protest against John Paul II's expected doctrinal texts (cf. D. Mieth, Kölner Erklärung, LThK, VI3, p. 196) [LTHK is the *Lexikon für Theologie und Kirche*, a German-language "Lexicon of Theology and the Church", whose editors included Karl Rahner and Cardinal Walter Kasper].

Pope John Paul II, who knew the situation of moral theology very well and followed it closely, commissioned work on an encyclical to set these things right again. It appeared on August 6, 1993, under the title *Veritatis splendor*, triggering vehement backlashes on the part of moral theologians. Already before this there was the *Catechism of the Catholic Church*, which persuasively and systematically presented morality as proclaimed by the Church.

I have not forgotten how then-leading German moral theologian Franz Böckle, having returned to his native Switzerland after retirement, made an announcement in anticipation of the judgments possibly contained in *Veritatis splendor*. He said that if the document should determine that there are actions which are always and under all circumstances to be classified as evil, he would speak out against it with all the energy at his disposal. The benevolent God spared him from carrying out this resolution; Böckle died on July 8, 1991. The encyclical was published on August 6, 1993, and did indeed include the judgment that there are actions which can never become good. The pope was fully aware of the weight of this decision at that moment, and for precisely this part of his text, he had again consulted leading specialists who had no part in the drafting of the encyclical. He knew that he must leave no doubt that a morality based on a calculation of relative goods [*die Moral der Güterabwägung*] must [in the end] respect a final boundary. There are goods that are never subject to such a calculus. There are values that must never be abandoned for the sake of a higher one, values that even surpass the preservation of physical life. There is martyrdom. God is more—more even than physical survival. A life bought with the denial of God, a life based on an ultimate lie, is a non-life. Martyrdom is a fundamental category of Christian existence. In the theory advocated by Böckle and many others, martyrdom is no longer morally necessary, and this fact shows that the very essence of Christianity is at stake in this dispute.

In moral theology, of course, another question had meanwhile become pressing. A certain hypothesis gained widespread acceptance, namely that the Magisterium of the Church should have definitive competence ("infallibility") only in matters concerning the Faith itself, that moral questions could not be a matter for the infallible decisions of the Magisterium. There is probably something correct in this hypothesis that warrants further discussion. But there is a moral minimum [*ein Minimum morale*: apparently a Germanization of the Latin *minimum morale*] that is indissolubly linked to the fundamental decision of faith and must be defended if faith is not to be reduced to a theory but rather recognized in its claim on concrete life. All this makes apparent just how fundamentally the Church's authority in moral matters is being called into question. Whoever denies the Church a final teaching competence in this domain forces her to remain silent precisely at the point where the boundary between truth and lie is at stake.

Independently of this question, there was a hypothesis expounded in many moral theological circles that the Church does not and cannot have her own morality. It was argued that all moral propositions would also know parallels in other religions and therefore a Christian *proprium* [a distinctively Christian morality] cannot exist. However, the question of the *proprium* of a biblical morality is not answered by the fact that for each single proposition, a parallel can be found in other religions as well. Rather, the question regards biblical morality as a whole, which as such is something new and different with respect to its individual parts.

In the end, what is unique about the moral doctrine of Holy Scripture is that it is anchored in the image of God, in faith toward the one God, who manifested himself in Jesus Christ and lived as man. The Decalogue [the Ten Commandments] is an application to human life of biblical faith in God. Morality and the image of God belong together, and together they result in that unique innovation of the Christian attitude toward the world and toward human life. Moreover, Christianity has been described from the beginning with the word *hodós* [Greek for "road"]. Faith is a

path and a way to live. In the old Church, the cate-
chumenate was created as a living space set apart from
an increasingly demoralized culture, a space in which
that distinctive innovation of the Christian way of life
was practiced and, at the same time, protected from
the common mode of living. I think that even today
something like catechumenal communities are needed,
so that Christian life, with all its character, can hold its
own ground.

II. Initial Reactions in the Church

1.

As I have tried to show, the unraveling of the Christian
understanding of morality—an ongoing process that
was long in preparation—attained an unprecedented
radicality in the 1960s. This confusion concerning the
Church's moral teaching authority was bound to have
an effect on her various spheres of life. In the context of the meeting of episcopal conference presidents
from across the world with Pope Francis [which took
place February 21–24, 2019, at the Vatican], the question of priestly life, as well as seminaries, is of particular interest. When it comes to the issue of seminary
preparation for the priestly ministry, one can indeed
note a widespread breakdown from the earlier form of
this preparation.

In various seminaries, homosexual cliques rose up that acted more or less openly and that markedly changed the climate in these seminaries. In one seminary in southern Germany, candidates for the priesthood lived together with candidates for the lay pastoral ministry. At the common meals, seminarians and lay pastors—sometimes accompanied by their wives and children, sometimes by their girlfriends—all ate together. The climate in this seminary could not facilitate preparation for the priestly office. The Holy See knew of such problems, without having precise information. As a first step, an Apostolic Visitation to United States seminaries was ordered.

Since the criteria for the selection and appointment of bishops had been changed after the Second Vatican Council, the relationship of bishops to their seminaries was also very different. Now the main criterion for the appointment of new bishops was seen to be their "conciliarity", which of course could be understood to mean very different things. In fact, in many parts of the Church, the conciliar attitude was understood as a critical or negative approach to the hitherto existing tradition, which was now to be replaced by a new, radically open relationship with the world. One bishop, who had previously been a seminary rector, arranged for the seminarians to be shown pornographic films, supposedly with the intention of making them thereby resistant to behavior contrary to the Faith. There were individual bishops—not only in the United States of America— who rejected the Catholic tradition altogether and strove to cultivate a kind of new, modern "Catholicity" in their dioceses. Perhaps it is worth mentioning that in not a few seminaries, students caught reading my books were considered unsuitable for the priesthood. My books were hidden away like naughty literature and only read, as it were, under the desk.

The Apostolic Visitation that took place at this point brought no new findings, apparently because various powers had joined together to conceal the real situation. A second Visitation was ordered, which brought to light considerably more information, but on the whole failed to achieve any results. To be sure, since the 1970s, the situation in seminaries has generally improved. Still, a new strengthening of priestly vocations came about only in a scattered manner, as the overall situation had taken a different turn.

2.

The question of pedophilia, as I recall, did not become acute until the second half of the 1980s. By then, it had already grown into a public issue in the United States, to the point that the bishops sought help in Rome, since canon law, as written in the new [1983] Code, did not seem adequate for taking the necessary measures. Rome and the Roman canonists at first had a hard time with these concerns; in their opinion, temporary suspension from priestly office had to be sufficient for bringing about purification and clarification. This could not be accepted by the American bishops, because the priests in this state remained in the service of the bishop and thus could be taken to be [still] directly associated with him. A renewal and deepening of the new Code's criminal law, deliberately constructed in a loose way, could move ahead only at a slow pace.

In addition, however, there was a fundamental problem in the understanding of criminal law. Only so-called *garantismo* ["guarantism", a kind of procedural protectionism, featured in the Italian constitution] was still regarded as "conciliar". This means that above all else the rights of the accused had to be guaranteed, to an extent that, in practice, ruled out conviction altogether. As a counterweight to the often inadequate defense options available to the accused, their right to defense in the sense of *garantismo* was stretched so far that convictions were hardly possible anymore.

Allow me a brief excursus at this point. In light of the extent of pedophilic misconduct, a saying of Jesus has again come to mind: "Whoever causes one of these little ones who believe in me to sin, it would be better for him if a great millstone were hung round his neck and he were thrown into the sea" (Mk 9:42). In its original sense, this saying does not refer to the sexual seduction of children. The phrase "little ones" means, in Jesus' language, simple believers who, through the intellectual pride of people who think themselves smart, can be led to fall in their faith. So here Jesus protects the deposit of the Faith with an emphatic threat of punishment against those who do it harm. The modern application of the sentence is not in itself wrong, but it must not obscure the original meaning. Contrary to any *garantismo*, this original sense makes patently clear that it is not only the right of the accused which matters and requires a guarantee. Other great goods, such as the Faith, are just as important.

A balanced canon law corresponding to the whole of Jesus' message must therefore not only provide a guarantee for the accused, the respect for whom is a legal good. It must also protect the Faith, which is just as important a legal asset. A properly formed canon law must therefore contain a double guarantee: legal protection of the accused, legal protection of the good at stake. When one proposes this notion today, so clear in itself, one's words generally fall on deaf ears when it comes to protecting the Faith as a legal good. In the common understanding of the law [*Rechtsbewußtsein*], the Faith no longer seems to have the status of a good to be protected. This is an alarming situation that the pastors of the Church must bear in mind and take seriously.

Adding to these brief notes on the situation of priestly formation at the time of the public outbreak of the crisis, I would now like to make a few remarks regarding the development of canon law on this matter. In principle, it is the Congregation of the Clergy that is responsible for dealing with crimes committed by priests. But since *garantismo* largely prevailed at the time, I agreed with Pope John Paul II that it was appropriate to assign the competence for these offences to the Congregation for the Doctrine of the Faith, under the title *Delicta maiora contra fidem* ["Major offense against the Faith"].

This arrangement also made it possible to impose the maximum penalty, in other words, expulsion from the clergy, which could not have been imposed under other legal provisions. This was not a ploy to gain the ability to impose the maximum penalty; rather, it follows as a consequence of the gravity of the Faith for the Church. Indeed, it is important to see that such misconduct by clerics ultimately damages the Faith: such offenses are possible only where faith no longer determines the actions of man. The severity of the punishment, however, also presupposes a clear proof of the offense—this aspect of *garantismo* remains legitimate. In other words, in order to impose the maximum penalty lawfully, a genuine criminal process is required. But both the dioceses and the Holy See were overwhelmed by this requirement. Thus we drafted a minimal form of criminal proceedings and left open the eventuality that the Holy See itself would take over the trial when the diocese or the metropolitan administration is unable to do so. In each case, the trial would have to be reviewed by the Congregation for the Doctrine of the Faith in order to guarantee the rights of the accused. Finally, in the Feria IV (i.e., the assembly of the members of the Congregation), we established an appellate court to provide for the possibility of an appeal. Because all of this really went beyond the capacities of the Congregation for the Doctrine of the Faith, and because delays began arising that needed to be prevented, given the nature of the matter, Pope Francis has since undertaken further reforms.

III.

1.

What must we do? Perhaps in order to set things right we should create another Church? Well, that experiment has already been made and has already failed. Only obedience to and love for our Lord Jesus Christ can point out the right way. So let us first try to understand, anew and from within [ourselves], what the Lord wanted and wants with us.

First, I would say: If we really wanted to summarize very briefly the content of the Faith as the Bible lays it down, we might say that the Lord has entered into a story of love with us and wants to subsume all creation in it. Ultimately, the counterforce against the evil that threatens us and the whole world can only consist in our entering into this love. This is the real counterforce against evil. The power of evil arises from our refusal to love God. He who entrusts himself to the love of God is redeemed. Our not being redeemed is a consequence of our inability to love God. Learning to love God is therefore the path of human redemption.

Let us now try to unpack a little further this essential content of God's revelation. We might say that the first fundamental gift faith offers us is the certainty that God exists. A world without God can only be a world without meaning. For where does it all come from, everything that is? It has no spiritual ground anyway [many think]. It is somehow simply there and has neither any goal nor any meaning. There are, then, no standards of good or evil. Only what is stronger than the other can prevail, and power is the only principle. Truth does not matter; it does not even exist. Yet, only if things have a spiritual ground, if things are willed and thought out—only if there is a Creator God who is good and wills the good—can the life of man, too, have meaning.

The existence of God as creator and measure of all things is first and foremost a primordial need. But a God who did not express himself at all, who did not make himself known, would remain a conjecture and therefore could not determine the shape [*Gestalt*] of our life. For God to be really God in this deliberate creation, we must expect that he will express himself in some form. He has done so in many ways, but he did it decisively in the call that went to Abraham, giving those in search of God the[ir] orientation, which leads beyond all expectation: God himself becomes creature, speaks as man with us men.

In this way, the sentence "God is" ultimately becomes a truly joyous message, precisely because he is more than knowledge, because he creates love and is love. Making people once more aware of this is the first and fundamental task entrusted to us by the Lord.

A society where God is absent, a society that does not know him and treats him as nonexistent, is a society that loses its measure. In our day, the catchphrase of God's death gained currency. When God dies in a society—we were assured—it becomes free. In reality, the death of God in a society also means the end of freedom, because what dies is the meaning that gives it orientation, and because the measure that points us in the right direction by teaching us to distinguish good from evil disappears. Western society is a society in which God is absent in the public sphere and to which, it is thought, God has nothing left to say. And that is why it is a society in which the measure of what is human dwindles away more and more. At some point, it becomes suddenly perceptible that what is evil and destroys man has become a commonplace. So it is with pedophilia. Proffered only recently as a fully legitimate practice, it has spread further and further. And now we are shocked to realize that things are happening to our children and young people which threaten to destroy them. The fact that this could spread even in the Church and among priests ought particularly to disturb us.

How could pedophilia reach such proportions? In the last analysis, the reason lies in the absence of God. Even we Christians and priests prefer not to talk about God, since this kind of talk does not seem practical. After the shock of the Second World War, we in Germany had still expressly framed our constitution with responsibility before God, as a guiding principle. Half a century later, it was no longer possible to include responsibility before God as a measure in the European constitution. God is seen as the concern of a small special interest group, and he can no longer stand as measure for the community as a whole. This decision reflects the situation in the West, where God has become the private affair of a minority.

One paramount task that must follow from the moral shocks of our time is that of beginning once again—we ourselves—to live by God and unto him. Above all, we ourselves must learn again to recognize God as the foundation of our life instead of leaving him aside as a somewhat fictitious cliché. I still remember the warning that the great theologian Hans Urs von Balthasar once wrote to me on one of his lettercards. "The triune God, Father, Son and Holy Spirit—do not presuppose him [*voraussetzen*], but present him [*vorsetzen*]!" Indeed, even in theology God is often presupposed as a matter of course, without dealing with him in the concrete. The subject of God seems so unreal, so far removed from the things that concern us. And yet, everything changes if one presents God instead of presupposing him, if one does not leave him somewhat in the background, but instead recognizes him as the center of one's thoughts, words, and actions.

2.

God became man for us. Man, his creature, is so close to his heart that he has united himself with him and has thus entered human history in a wholly practical way. He speaks with us, he lives with us, he suffers with us, and he took death upon himself for us. We talk about this in theology at great length, with scholarly words and ideas. But it is in precisely this way that we run the risk of becoming masters of the Faith instead of letting ourselves *be* renewed and mastered *by* it.

Let us consider this with regard to one central issue, the celebration of the Holy Eucharist. Our handling of the Eucharist can only arouse concern. The Second Vatican Council was rightly focused on returning this sacrament of the Presence of the Body and Blood of Christ, of the Presence of his Person, of his Passion, Death and Resurrection, once again to the center of Christian life and of the Church's very existence. In part, this really has come about, and we should be most grateful to the Lord for it.

And yet a rather different attitude predominates by far: not a new reverence for the presence of Christ's Death and Resurrection, but a way of dealing with him that destroys the greatness of the Mystery. Declining participation in the Sunday eucharistic celebration shows how little we Christians of today are still able to appreciate the greatness of this gift, which consists in his Real Presence. The Eucharist is degraded to a mere ceremonial gesture when one takes as a given the polite requirement that the Sacrament be offered, at family celebrations or occasions such as weddings and funerals, to every person invited for family reasons. That Mass attendees in some places receive the

Holy Sacrament as a matter of course demonstrates that many see Communion as a purely ceremonial gesture. Thus, when we think on what is to be done, it becomes clear that we do not need another Church of our own design. Rather, what we need above all is a renewal of faith in the reality of Jesus Christ given to us in the Blessed Sacrament.

In conversations with victims of pedophilia, I have been made ever more acutely aware of this necessity. A young woman who had [formerly] served as an altar girl told me that her superior, the chaplain, always introduced the sexual abuse he committed against her with the words: "This is my body which will be given up for you." It is obvious that this woman can no longer hear the words of Consecration without re-experiencing all the horrific agony of her abuse. Yes, we must urgently implore the Lord for forgiveness, and above all else we must invoke him and ask him to teach us all anew to understand the magnitude of his suffering, his sacrifice. And we must do all we can to protect the gift of the Holy Eucharist from abuse.

3.

Finally, there is the mystery of the Church. I still remember the sentence with which Romano Guardini, some one hundred years ago, expressed the joyful hope that was pressing in on him and many others: "An event of inestimable importance has begun; the

Church is awakening in souls." By this he meant that
the Church was no longer experienced and perceived
merely as an external apparatus entering our lives, as a
kind of authority, but rather was beginning to be perceived as becoming present within people's hearts—as
something not merely external, but affecting us inter-
nally. About half a century later, reconsidering this process and looking at just what was happening [in the
world], I felt tempted to reverse the sentence: "The
Church is dying in souls." Indeed, the Church today is
widely regarded as just some kind of political apparatus.
One speaks of it almost exclusively in terms of political categories, and this holds even with bishops, who
largely formulate their vision of the Church of tomorrow exclusively in political terms. The crisis, brought
on by the many cases of clerical abuse, tempts us to
regard the Church as something almost unacceptable,
which we must now take into our own hands and rede-
sign from the ground up. However, a Church that we
build can offer no hope.

Jesus himself compared the Church to a fishing net
in which good and bad fish are ultimately separated by
God himself. There is also the parable of the Church as
a field in which grows the good grain that God himself
has sown, but so do the weeds that "an enemy" has
covertly sown in it. Indeed, the weeds in God's field,
the Church, are exceedingly visible, and the bad fish
in the net likewise show their strength. Nevertheless,
the field is still God's field and the net is God's fishing

net. In every age, there are not only the weeds and the evil fish, but also the seeds of God and the good fish. Proclaiming both with emphasis is not a false form of apologetics, but a necessary service to the truth. On this point, it is necessary to refer to an important text in the Revelation of Saint John. There, the devil is identified as the accuser who day and night accuses our brothers before God (12:10). Saint John's Apocalypse thus takes up a thought central to the frame story in the Book of Job (Job 1; 2:1–10; 42:7–16). There, the devil talks to God and tries to dismiss Job's righteousness as being purely external. This is exactly what the Apocalypse has to say: the devil wants to prove that there is no righteous man, that all man's righteousness is just an outward display; if one could hew closer to a person, then the appearance of righteousness would quickly fall away.

The narrative in Job begins with a dispute between God and the devil after God refers to Job as a truly righteous man. Job is now to be put to the test, in order to see who is right. Take away his possessions, argues the devil, and you will see that none of his piety remains. God lets him make this attempt, and Job does well. Then the devil pushes on and says: "Skin for skin! All that a man has he will give for his life. But put forth your hand now, and touch his bone and his flesh, and he will curse you to your face" (Job 2:4f.). God grants the devil a second try. He may touch Job's skin as well. The only thing he may not do is kill the man. For Christians, it is clear that this Job, standing before God as an exemplar of all mankind, is Jesus Christ. In Saint John's Apocalypse, the drama of humanity is presented to us in all its breadth. The Creator God is confronted with the devil who speaks ill of all mankind and all creation. He says, not only to God but above all to man: *Look at what this God has done. Supposedly a good creation, but really it's full of misery and disgust.* In reality, this disparagement of creation is a disparagement of God. It wants to prove that God himself is not good, thus turning us away from him.

The relevance of what the Apocalypse is telling us here is obvious. Today, the accusation against God above all revolves around characterizing his Church as entirely bad and thereby turning us from her. The idea of a Church made better by our own hands is really a proposal of the devil, intended to turn us away from the living God, through a deceitful logic that we fall for far too easily. No, the Church—even today—is not just made up of bad fish and weeds. God's Church exists even today, and this very day she is the instrument by which God saves us. It is very important to contrast the lies and half-truths of the devil with the whole truth: Yes, there is sin in the Church and there is evil. But even today there also is the Holy Church, which is indestructible. Even today there are many people who humbly believe, suffer, and love, in whom the real God, the loving God, manifests himself to us. Even today God has his witnesses (*martyres*) in the world. We have only to be attentive in order to see and hear them.

The word "martyr" is taken from procedural law. In the trial against the devil, Jesus Christ is God's first and true witness, the first martyr, whom countless others have since followed. Today's Church is more than ever a Church of martyrs and thus a witness to the living God. Everywhere today—among ordinary people especially, but also in the high ranks of the Church—we can find witnesses who stand up for God with their life and suffering. The fact that we do not want to recognize them, is a sloth of the heart. One of the great essential tasks of our evangelization is, as far as we can, to create habitats of faith and above all to find and recognize them.

I live in a house, in a small community of people who discover such witnesses of the living God time and again in everyday life, pointing them out to me with joy. To see and find the living Church is a wonderful task that strengthens us and makes us rejoice ever anew in our Faith.

At the end of my reflections, I would like to thank Pope Francis for everything he is doing to show us, time and again, the light of God, which even today has not gone out. Thank you, Holy Father!